ID0787683

The History
of Nursing

Lizabeth Craig

LUCENT BOOKS

A part of Gale, Cengage Learning

Detroit • New York • San Francisco • New Haven, Conn • Waterville, Maine • London

CONCORDIA UNIVERSITY LIBRARY
PORTLAND, OR 97211

© 2014 Gale, Cengage Learning

ALL RIGHTS RESERVED. No part of this work covered by the copyright herein may be reproduced, transmitted, stored, or used in any form or by any means graphic, electronic, or mechanical, including but not limited to photocopying, recording, scanning, digitizing, taping, Web distribution, information networks, or information storage and retrieval systems, except as permitted under Section 107 or 108 of the 1976 United States Copyright Act, without the prior written permission of the publisher.

Every effort has been made to trace the owners of copyrighted material.

LIBRARY OF CONGRESS CATALOGING-IN-PUBLICATION DATA

Craig, Lizabeth.
  The history of nursing / by Lizabeth Craig.
    pages cm. -- (World history)
  Includes bibliographical references and index.
  ISBN 978-1-4205-0823-9 (hardcover)
  1. Nursing--History. I. Title.
  RT31.C73 2014
  610.73--dc23

                                                    2013021587

Lucent Books
27500 Drake Rd.
Farmington Hills, MI 48331

ISBN-13: 978-1-4205-0823-9
ISBN-10: 1-4205-0823-7

Printed in the United States of America
1 2 3 4 5 6 7 17 16 15 14 13

Contents

Foreword

Each year, on the first day of school, nearly every history teacher faces the task of explaining why his or her students should study history. Many reasons have been given. One is that lessons exist in the past from which contemporary society can benefit and learn. Another is that exploration of the past allows us to see the origins of our customs, ideas, and institutions. Concepts such as democracy, ethnic conflict, or even things as trivial as fashion or mores, have historical roots.

Reasons such as these impress few students, however. If anything, these explanations seem remote and dull to young minds. Yet history is anything but dull. And therein lies what is perhaps the most compelling reason for studying history: History is filled with great stories. The classic themes of literature and drama—love and sacrifice, hatred and revenge, injustice and betrayal, adversity and overcoming adversity—fill the pages of history books, feeding the imagination as well as any of the great works of fiction do.

The story of the Children's Crusade, for example, is one of the most tragic in history. In 1212 Crusader fever hit Europe. A call went out from the pope that all good Christians should journey to Jerusalem to drive out the hated Muslims and return the city to Christian control. Heeding the call, thousands of children made the journey. Parents bravely allowed many children to go, and entire communities were inspired by the faith of these small Crusaders. Unfortunately, many boarded ships were captained by slave traders, who enthusiastically sold the children into slavery as soon as they arrived at their destination. Thousands died from disease, exposure, and starvation on the long march across Europe to the Mediterranean Sea. Others perished at sea.

Another story, from a modern and more familiar place, offers a soul-wrenching view of personal humiliation but also the ability to rise above it. Hatsuye Egami was one of 110,000 Japanese Americans sent to internment camps during World War II. "Since yesterday we Japanese have ceased to be human beings," he wrote in his diary. "We are numbers. We are no longer Egamis, but the number 23324. A tag with that number is on every trunk, suitcase and bag. Tags, also, on our breasts." Despite such dehumanizing treatment, most internees worked hard to control their bitterness. They created workable communities inside the camps and demonstrated again and again their loyalty as Americans.

These are but two of the many stories from history that can be found in the pages of the Lucent Books World History series. All World History titles rely on sound research and verifiable evidence, and all give students a clear sense of time, place, and chronology through maps and timelines as well as text.

All titles include a wide range of authoritative perspectives that demonstrate the complexity of historical interpretation and sharpen the reader's critical thinking skills. Formally documented quotations and annotated bibliographies enable students to locate and evaluate sources, often instantaneously via the Internet, and serve as valuable tools for further research and debate.

Finally, Lucent's World History titles present rousing good stories, featuring vivid primary source quotations drawn from unique, sometimes obscure sources such as diaries, public records, and contemporary chronicles. In this way, the voices of participants and witnesses as well as important biographers and historians bring the study of history to life. As we are caught up in the lives of others, we are reminded that we too are characters in the ongoing human saga, and we are better prepared for our own roles.

Important Dates in the

c. 250 B.C.
King Asoka of India establishes the earliest known hospitals that employ people in a nursing role.

651
Hôtel Dieu is established in Paris, France.

c. 450
The Benedictine nursing order is founded.

1000s
Many military and religious orders are founded for care of the sick.

1348
The Alexian Brothers is founded for the care of plague victims.

1400s
The rise of nonreligious orders of nurses.

1873
Linda Richards becomes the first formally trained American nurse.

1860
Florence Nightingale establishes the first organized education program for nurses.

| B.C. 250 | A.D. 650 | 1050 | 1450 | 1850 |

A.D. 60
Christian deaconess Phoebe is credited with being the first visiting nurse.

300
The Parabolani brotherhood is founded for care of the sick and burial of the dead.

542
A plague pandemic wipes out almost half the population of Europe.

1207
The birth of Saint Elizabeth of Hungary, patron saint of nursing.

1633
Saint Vincent de Paul founds the Daughters (or Sisters) of Charity.

c. 1550–1850
The so-called dark period of nursing.

1853
The Crimean War begins.

1820
Birth of Florence Nightingale.

History of Nursing

1881
Clara Barton establishes the American Red Cross and serves as its first president.

1901
The American Army Nurse Corps becomes part of the Army Medical Department.

1938
The Nurses Memorial in Arlington National Cemetery is dedicated.

1942
Twenty-one Australian nurses are executed by Japanese troops during the Bangka Island massacre.

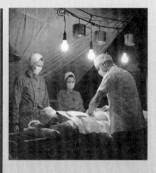

1945
Mobile Army Surgical Hospital (MASH) units are created.

1900	1925	1950	1975	2000

1908
First licensure law for nurses is passed in North Carolina.

1911
The American Nurses Association is founded.

1914–1918
World War I; a worldwide influenza pandemic kills millions.

1939–1945
World War II.

1950–1953
The Korean War.

1965
The first U.S. Army nurses begin serving in the Vietnam War.

1966
Men begin serving as U.S. Army nurses.

1971
The hospice movement is established by Florence Wald and associates.

1978
The International History of Nursing Society is formed.

2010
The Patient Protection and Affordable Health Care Act is passed by Congress; the Institute of Medicine releases *The Future of Nursing: Leading Change, Advancing Health* to address concerns for the future of nursing.

1980
The American Assembly of Men in Nursing is formed.

Introduction

The Finest Art

"Nursing is an art: and if it is to be made an art, it requires an exclusive devotion as hard a preparation, as any painter's or sculptor's work; for what is the having to do with dead canvas or dead marble, compared with having to do with the living body, the temple of God's spirit? It is one of the Fine Arts: I had almost said, the finest of Fine Arts."[1] So wrote Florence Nightingale (1820–1910), one of the most famous and influential nurses. The history of nursing is a long, colorful, and often emotionally moving story. Nursing as we know it today— a profession of well-trained individuals distinct from physicians—did not fully develop until the 1800s with the groundbreaking work of Nightingale, but the role of caregiver to the sick, injured, poor, and helpless has been a part of human existence since the appearance of the earliest human societies.

Health Care in Prehistoric Times

Little is known about health care among the most primitive of human societies. Early humans may have learned some of what they knew from observing how animals cared for their own injuries. Eventually, as humans attempted to explain the natural phenomena around them, including illness, a belief in the supernatural arose. Good and evil spirits, superstitions, rituals, spells, and various treatments such as trephination of the skull (drilling a hole in the skull to let out "evil spirits") became important parts of managing illness and expelling demons. As spiritual tradition became more complicated, certain members of the community came to be responsible for interpreting and practicing their beliefs. Medicine men and women, priest-physicians, or shamans became the principal healers for the group. Women were often responsible for preparing and applying the treatments, including herbal drugs and wound care.

As human civilizations developed, particularly in the Middle East, social institutions such as government, religion, codes of law and justice, and health care evolved. In Egypt a complex hierarchy of healers and system of medical care and surgery arose. Other ancient civilizations, such as Persia, Mesopotamia, Palestine, India, and China also had well-developed medical systems, based mostly on religion, magic, and superstition.

Ancient Greece and Rome

The evolution of health care from religious to rational began with ancient Greece. Scientific, observational, philosophical, and natural explanations began to replace the supernatural ones. The Greek philosopher-physician Hippocrates became one of the most influential thinkers of ancient history and is often called the Father of Medicine. Greek literature contains references to nurses, but mostly in the context of wet nurses and midwives. Nursing functions as they are known today were mostly performed by men or slaves, since women were expected to remain in the home and tend to their own families.

Ancient Rome also had a well-developed system of health care that was heavily dependent on the interventions of gods and goddesses. The Romans were innovators in the area of public health and hygiene. A class of male practitioners called *nosocomi* acted as nurses. Women, along with their slaves, attended to the sick in the home. After the Roman conquest of Greece, Greek influences were added as many Greek physicians became slaves. Galen, a Greek physician, was a prolific writer and skilled surgeon. Hippocratic and Galenic thought influenced later European medical thought for centuries as Christianity took hold and came to dominate Western life.

What Is a Nurse?

The word *nurse* has its roots in the Latin words *nutrire*, "to nourish," and *nutrix*, "nursing mother" or "one who nurses infants." The word first appeared in English in the thirteenth century and referred to a wet nurse, or a woman who suckled the infants of others. Later on, it referred to someone (usually a woman) who cared for children, and still later, to those who cared for the sick. Because these functions were traditionally carried out by women, nursing began to evolve as a role mainly for women. With the rise of Christianity, nursing began to establish itself as an institution distinct from medicine and physicians. In the eighteenth century *nursing* came to refer to one who carried out the functions of a nurse under the direction and supervision of a physician.

The function and role of the nurse has not always been fully appreciated, and there have been times in history when nurses and those who perform the functions of the nurse have been ignored, underappreciated, and even persecuted.

The Greek physician Galen was a skilled surgeon and a prolific writer on medical matters in the second century A.D.

Physician and writer Victor Robinson (1886–1947) wrote:

> Woman is an instinctive nurse, taught by Mother Nature. The nurse has always been a necessity, thus lacking in social status. In primitive times she was a slave, and in the civilized era a domestic. Overlooked in the plans of legislators, and forgotten in the curricula of pedagogues [educators], she was left without protection and remained without education. . . . Drawn from the nameless and numberless army of poverty, the nurse worked as a menial and obeyed as a servant. Denied the dignity of a trade, and devoid of professional ethics, she could not rise above the degradation of her environment. It never occurred to the [philosophers] of the past that it would be safer for the public welfare if nurses were educated instead of lawyers. The untrained nurse is as old as the human race; the trained nurse is a recent discovery. The distinction between the two is a sharp commentary on the follies and prejudices of mankind.[2]

Throughout the centuries and around the world, however, the knowledge, skills, and wisdom gained by caregivers of all kinds have grown and developed and have been passed on to successive generations, constantly expanding and improving over time.

The role of the nurse in modern times has continued to expand and has come to include literally hundreds of functions in health education, health promotion, and groundbreaking research, in addition to the traditional role as caregiver to the sick, injured, and dying. As human society progresses within the twenty-first century, the role of the nurse is stronger, more independent, and more valuable than ever before. Nurses can be found wherever human beings exist—from the slums of India or Brazil to the hallowed halls of the most prestigious universities in Europe or the United States, from the deserts of North Africa to the jungles of Asia and South America, in the home, hospital, laboratory, school, community, and battlefield. "Whatever tomorrow's demands," writes nursing historian Mary Ellen Snodgrass, "unknown contagion, breakdown of social structures, violence, and natural disaster—nursing will reshape, realign, and replot the most humane methods of uplifting mankind."[3]

Chapter One

A Religious Calling

Organized nursing has its roots in the emergence of Christianity as a guiding force in everyday life. At the beginning of the Christian era, more than two thousand years ago, the Roman Empire controlled most of Europe and parts of Asia and Africa. Rome was at the height of its power when a carpenter named Jesus of Nazareth was born in Judea. As an adult, Jesus became a prophet and teacher, with a message of forgiveness of sins and everlasting life in heaven for those who followed him. The message was very attractive for people who lived under the oppression of the Roman Empire, and after Jesus's death in about A.D. 33, his disciples, or close followers, spread his message throughout the empire, winning converts and establishing Christian churches around the Mediterranean area.

In 312 the Roman emperor Constantine converted to Christianity. The following year he established Christianity as the official religion of the empire. By this time, the empire had begun to decline in power because of political conflicts, economic crises, and invasions by warlike tribes from northern Europe. As the empire declined, Christianity continued to spread and gain strength. By 400 it had grown from a simple religion into a very complex one, with many rituals and ceremonies, strict rules for the conduct of daily life, and a structured hierarchy of priests, bishops, and other officials.

Nursing and Early Christianity

One of the foundations of early Christian teaching was the importance of love and mercy for one's fellow humans. Care for those who were suffering became a spiritual act. Based on biblical scriptures, the church established seven Corporal Works of Mercy—feed the hungry, give drink to the thirsty, clothe the naked, shelter the homeless, visit the sick, visit those in prison, and bury the dead. Nursing historian M. Patricia Donahue writes:

> From the earliest point in its history, the Christian Church assumed the care of the sick, the poor, and the helpless. This activity was in keeping with Christ's refusal to accept human suffering. Other religions had viewed suffering as deserved. . . . Christ specialized in relieving it. Thus spiritual meaning became attached to the care given to humanity and to the suffering endured by it. The care of the sick and distressed became an avowed duty of all Christian men and women.[4]

In the Middle Ages care of the sick became an avowed duty of all Christian men and women.

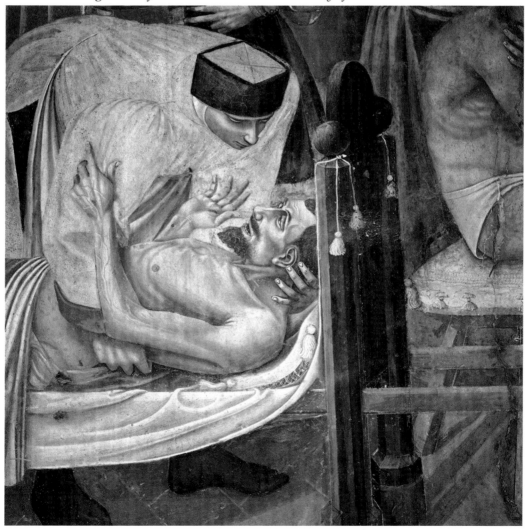

Christian teaching held that women were equal to men in the sight of God and therefore could participate alongside men in God's work. The elevation of care of the poor and sick to a spiritual calling provided women, especially unmarried women, with a respectable function outside the home. Several different groups of women within the church provided care to the sick. These groups included widows, deaconesses, and matrons.

Widows were officers in the early church with special duties involving care of the sick and the poor. At that time, the word *widow* did not necessarily mean a woman whose husband had died; it could also refer to a woman who was older (most were more than sixty years old) and had earned respect. Widows sometimes lived in monasteries (religious communities), but they might also live in their own homes. They took vows of chastity and could not marry. By the third century, widows in monasteries became known as nuns.

Deaconesses were also officers of the church. Only unmarried women or widows could be deaconesses. Many of them were educated, well-to-do women who might be relatives of wealthy landowners or of high-ranking male church officers such as bishops. Deaconesses had several duties within the church and the community, including care of the sick and charity work for the poor. Deaconesses were often in charge of early institutions of care, called by the Greek name *xenodocheia* (zeno-DO-kee-ia), the forerunners of today's hospitals. These institutions took in all kinds of people who needed help—the sick, the poor, the homeless, the disabled, the mentally ill, orphans, and travelers. They also included housing and offices for the physicians and nurses who worked there. Eventually, the *xenodocheia* became specialized, with separate areas for each kind of need. The wards for the sick were called *nosochomia* (no-so-KO-mia).

Matrons were upper-class Roman women who had converted to Christianity and participated in public service in various ways, which often included care of the sick and the poor. Some matrons chose to give up their wealth for the sake of charity work, such as Marcella, who converted her palace in the center of Rome into a monastery, and Fabiola, who gave all her wealth to the poor and started a free hospital in her home after the death of her second husband.

Nursing in the Early Middle Ages

The "Middle Ages" is the name given to the roughly one thousand years from the fall of the Roman Empire in A.D. 476 until about 1500. By 480 the empire had lost almost all its power and influence in Europe. Europe entered a period of social decay commonly known as the Dark Ages, a period of about five hundred years from the fall of the empire to about 1000. During this time, the learning and knowledge of art, science, and philosophy of the ancient Greeks and Romans was largely forgotten. It was a time of wars, epidemics of disease, natural disasters, and poverty. Cities

Religion and Medicine in the Middle Ages

In the Dark Ages after the fall of the Roman Empire, Europeans abandoned much of the learning that had been achieved by the ancient Greeks and Romans. People tended to blame illness on demons, curses, and superstitious pagan beliefs. Illness was treated with spells, magic, or homemade potions. The few physicians of the time still held to the old Greek ideas about illness being caused by an imbalance of four main body fluids, which they called humors: black bile, yellow bile, blood, and phlegm. Health could be regained by restoring balance in the humors through diet, exercise, rest, herbal remedies, and bloodletting, the practice of cutting a vein to let blood out in an effort to restore balance.

As Christianity spread and gained influence in Europe, ideas and attitudes about health and illness began to come from church authorities. Illness and suffering were seen as the result of sinfulness by the sufferer, or as a divine test of religious faith. The church declared many traditional healing practices illegal; these were replaced with "acceptable" Christian alternatives, such as constant prayer to the saints or belief in divine intervention by God. Dissection was outlawed, so very little was learned about the inner workings of the human body. Although suffering was seen as having a divine purpose, the church also taught that the body belonged to God and therefore must be properly cared for. This idea led to the rise of monastic centers of care for the sick, the poor, and others in need.

declined, and trade with other parts of the world disappeared. There were no real countries with defined borders like the modern nations of today. Instead, large territories of land, occupied by warlike tribes such as the Visigoths, Burgundians, Slavs, Saxons, and Franks, were governed by kings who fought constantly with each other for more land and more power.

European people were divided into three main groups. Most were serfs—poverty-stricken farmers who worked the land but did not own it. Much of the land was divided into large holdings called manors, owned by the second group, the wealthy lords of the manor. The lord provided protection for the serfs living on his land, and the serfs served as soldiers for the lord if he went to war. This kind of economic system was called the feudal system. The third group was the clergy, or religious people such as bishops, priests, monks, and nuns.

As the Roman Empire declined, the Christian Church strengthened and became highly organized and quite wealthy. The church owned much of the land not already owned by the lords. It built large religious centers called monasteries. Many people chose to enter monasteries and spend their entire lives there, not only as a way to serve God, but also to escape the difficulties and hardships of worldly life and to find security and safety. Eventually, the church gained almost complete control over the everyday lives of the people, including care of the sick.

Monastic Orders

As membership in the clergy grew throughout the fourth and fifth centuries, its members became organized into communities called orders. The members of each order lived in the monastery and were governed by a strict set of rules, drawn up by the founder of the order. Three early orders included the Basilians, founded by Basil of Caesarea (330–379); the Augustinians, dedicated to Augustine of Hippo (354–430); and the Benedictines, founded by Benedict of Nursia (480–543).

Monastic orders brought back some of the civilization that had been lost in the early Middle Ages. Benedictine monks, for example, improved farming techniques, wrote histories of their lives, opened schools, and learned new ways to use herbs and other natural sub-

The religious order of Augustinian sisters operated an early hospital at Hôtel Dieu in Paris that opened in 651.

stances as medicines. Care of the sick and the poor became a main concern for the Benedictines; the first rule of Saint Benedict states, "Before all things and above all things care must be taken of the sick."[5] Some orders ran hospitals in the towns. Most of the medical and nursing care in institutions outside the monasteries was done by monks and nuns from the order, assisted by people from the community.

Monastic orders for women developed along with orders for men, especially during the fifth and sixth centuries. Women of all classes and social levels entered monastic life for various reasons, including security, the opportunity for education, and the chance to pursue a career or personal interest such as politics, literature, or medicine. Many of these monasteries, such as the one founded by Saint Radegunde (519–587) in Poitiers, France, were devoted almost entirely to care of the sick. An order of Augustinian sisters operated one of the most famous early hospitals, the Hôtel Dieu in Paris, France, which opened in 651.

Military Nursing Orders

Since the crucifixion of Christ, Christian people had been making pilgrimages (journeys to a sacred place) to the area where he lived and preached, an area known as the Holy Land (roughly the area of modern-day Israel). In the late eleventh century, a group called the Seljuk Turks, who were of the Muslim faith, took control of Jerusalem, a holy city to the Christians, and began persecuting and killing

Christians there. In response Pope Urban II called on Christian nations to send soldiers to the area to regain control of the Holy Land and Jerusalem. Men of all kinds participated—professional soldiers, members of the clergy, devout Christian people, and others simply looking for adventure or escape from trouble at home. These military and religious expeditions were called Crusades. Altogether, there were eight Crusades between 1096 and 1291.

The Crusades presented the need for more hospitals and more people to provide care for pilgrims traveling between Europe and the Holy Land. Injuries from battle, as well as diseases carried back and forth across Europe, led to the establishment of hospitals and of military nursing orders, called hospitallers, to provide care for the sick and injured. These orders were made up of three classes of men—knights, priests, and serving brothers. The knights were mostly upper-class men who had served as soldiers, protecting pilgrims to the Holy Land and fighting in the Crusades. The priests saw to the religious aspects of the order. The serving brothers took care of travelers. All three groups participated in nursing care of sick and injured people.

Three military nursing orders became famous for their work. The Knights Hospitallers of Saint John and Jerusalem served in a hospital for men called the Hospital of Saint John, established in Amalfi, Italy, in about 1050. This hospital, as well as one for women called the Hospital of Saint Mary Magdalene, had

During the Crusades, the Knights Hospitallers established hospitals in Malta, Italy, and Jerusalem.

on the island of Malta called the Sacra Infermeria, which became one of the best hospitals in Europe.

The Knights of Saint Lazarus of Jerusalem was also founded in the eleventh century. This order took on as its special service care of those with the skin disease leprosy. Leprosy was greatly feared in medieval times because it caused severe disfigurement of the face and other body parts, was incurable, and was (incorrectly) thought to be easily spread. For these reasons, lepers (those with leprosy) were shunned by society. The order was unique in that its members were crusaders who had contracted leprosy themselves. They built hospitals for lepers outside the walls of Jerusalem and Acre, a Muslim city in the Holy Land that was the site of several battles during the Crusades. The order eventually established leper hospitals all over Europe, but by the thirteenth century, leprosy had become less common, so the order turned more of its attention to military work rather than medical care.

The Teutonic Knights were an order of German knights formed in 1191 by German pilgrims to the Holy Land. They also built a hospital outside the city of Acre. As soon as a person joined the order, he would take a vow to care for the sick. Like the Hospitallers of Saint John, the Teutonic Knights also became wealthy after the Crusades and were given control of many hospitals in Germany. Their care was not as good as the hospitallers, however, and by the fourteenth century they had disbanded.

been originally established to take care of any person who needed help, but during the Crusades, both hospitals became occupied by wounded and sick crusaders. A branch of the hospitallers for women, called the Hospitaller Dames of the Order of Saint John of Jerusalem, served in the women's hospital. The care given by these two groups was so good that the order became quite wealthy from gifts given by grateful patients. After the Crusades, the order moved from place to place, changing its name depending on where it was headquartered. In 1575 it established a hospital

Mendicant and Secular Orders

Another type of order, called mendicant orders, also developed to serve the sick and the poor. Mendicants (from the Latin word *mendicare* meaning "to beg") were people who believed that the best way to serve God was to give up all worldly possessions and live in total poverty. They owned no land

Saint Francis of Assisi

Francis of Assisi (1181–1226) was the founder of the Franciscan order in the Christian Church. His father was a wealthy cloth merchant in Assisi, in the Italian province Perugia, but Francis showed little interest either in the family business or in his education, preferring to spend his days living the carefree life. He was handsome, charming, and spoiled by his parents. He decided to become a knight, but during an unsuccessful battle with a neighboring province, he was captured and became very ill from being held prisoner for more than a year. His illness caused him to think more about eternity and the fate of his soul after death. After having a dream in which he was visited by God, he gave up his expensive clothes and wasteful ways, began giving large amounts of family money and property to the poor, and adopted a life of poverty. His father was furious with Francis's behavior, so Francis gave up his inheritance and left home.

On his own, Francis traveled the countryside, ministering to the poor and ill. He felt particular compassion for lepers and visited them frequently, which caused the

people of his town to persecute him and treat him like a madman. Even so, he eventually gathered around him a group of followers, and in 1210 they traveled to Rome to ask Pope Innocent III to let them form an order. With the pope's approval, the Franciscans grew quickly. They took vows of complete poverty, living as mendicants, or beggars. In 1219 Francis went to Egypt and tried (unsuccessfully) to convert the Muslim sultan of Egypt to Christianity. In the years that followed, Francis suffered a series of health problems, including a blinding eye disease. He died in 1226 and was declared a saint by Pope Gregory IX in 1228.

Francis of Assisi founded the Franciscan order, probably the most famous mendicant order, in the early thirteenth century.

The Black Death

The Black Death is the name given to the pandemic of a disease called bubonic plague, which swept through Europe in the mid-1300s. It began in China and moved rapidly westward, carried by flea-infested rats that traveled with merchants on their ships and caravans. It arrived in Italy in 1347. From there it spread across Europe in a matter of months. Death came very quickly to those infected with the illness, and the symptoms were terrifying. It would start with a high fever, followed by severe stomach pain, coughing up blood, and the growth of large, pus-filled lumps under the armpits and in the groin called "buboes." Death quickly resulted from overwhelming fever, organ failure, or bleeding to death. Those who managed to avoid infection were so afraid of getting sick that stricken family members were often abandoned. In some places whole towns were wiped out. The numbers of dead soon overwhelmed the ability of the living to bury them, and bodies piled up in the streets.

Physicians were powerless to stop the disease or to help its victims. No one knew what caused the disease or how to treat it. The traditional Greek ideas about illness could not explain the vast numbers of people, even very healthy people, who were getting sick and dying. The church's traditional explanation for disease as punishment for sin was also useless, because all kinds of people—good, bad, religious, nonreligious—were falling ill and dying. People lost faith in both doctors and the church and turned back to superstition, astrology, and magic in a desperate attempt to avoid or cure the disease. By the time the plague finally subsided in the early 1350s, it had killed almost one-fourth of the population of Europe—more than 60 million people. The Black Death had important and lasting effects on how people thought about religion, medicine, and society in general.

and had no homes. They did not live in monasteries. They lived and served out in the world, traveling from place to place, and were completely dependent on the charity of others. There were five main mendicant orders, all founded in the thirteenth century—the Franciscans, Carmelites, Dominicans, Servites, and a branch of Augustinians. The Poor Clares, a part of the Franciscan order, was a mendicant order for nuns.

Secular nursing orders were semireligious groups whose members did not take religious vows and were not bound by the rules of any particular religious order. They served the sick, the poor, and orphans in their own communities. One secular order for men, called the Hospital Brothers of Saint Anthony, served those who suffered from a disease called ergotism, or Saint Anthony's Fire, which causes seizures, hallucinations, gangrene, and other severe symptoms. Another secular order, called the Alexian Brothers, was founded in Netherlands in 1348 to nurse victims of the Black Death, the worldwide pandemic of bubonic plague that killed millions, and to see to the burial of those who died. A secular order for women was called the Beguines. Members were of all classes, from rich to poor. Small groups of women would live together in houses called beguinages, situated near a church or a hospital, and care for the sick in homes and hospitals. Some groups of Beguines built their own hospitals.

Out of the Dark Ages

The final centuries of the Middle Ages were a time of tremendous social change. The failure of both religion and medicine to help people during the Black Death had caused people to question the authority of both groups. The feudal system declined, and a middle class began to grow. Cities began a period of growth and renewal. Large universities were established, became seats of learning and inquiry, and stimulated new ways of thinking about science, medicine, politics, religion, social justice, economics,

The Renaissance saw physicians like Andreas Vesalius, shown here teaching anatomy, make advances in the knowledge of the structure and function of the human body.

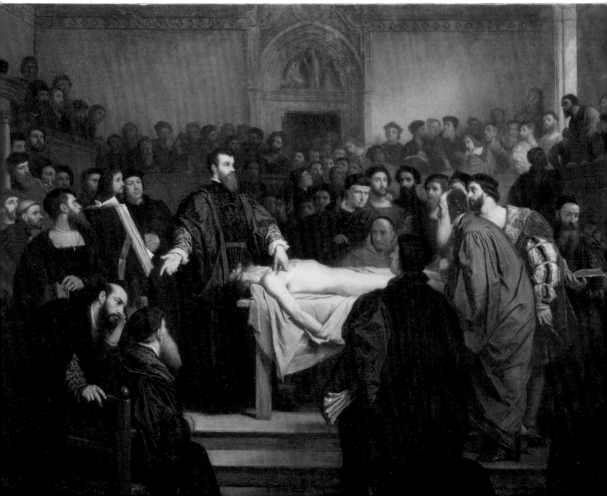

art, literature, and many other aspects of human society and the natural world.

This transitional period from the Middle Ages to modern times is called the Renaissance, a French word meaning "rebirth" or "renewal." It began in Italy in the late 1300s, spread throughout Europe, and lasted for about three hundred years. As the power of the church declined, interest in more worldly things rose. While the Christian faith remained very important in everyday life, intellectual people began to study the natural world from a more scientific point of view, and scientists such as Nicolaus Copernicus, Galileo Galilei, and Isaac Newton discovered new ways of looking at and learning about the world that were not determined by religion. There was a new interest in the human body for its beauty and form, expressed in Renaissance art and sculpture.

In medicine physicians such as Andreas Vesalius, Ambroise Paré, and William Harvey made great strides in learning more about the structure and function of the human body.

Religious restrictions that had forbidden dissections and autopsies (examination of the inside of a body after death) were relaxed, and these procedures provided a wealth of new information about internal human anatomy. New inventions, such as the microscope and thermometer, provided more information about the structure and function of the body. Physicians began to think more scientifically and conducted experiments to prove or disprove what they believed about illness.

The Protestant Reformation

One of the most important events of the Renaissance period to affect nursing care

City hospitals after the Protestant Reformation were dark, filthy, and poorly run.

was the Protestant Reformation. The Reformation began in 1517 and was led by a German monk named Martin Luther (1483–1546). It began as an attempt to reform the Christian Church, which many clergy members felt had become corrupt. In addition, new ideas about the proper role of religion in everyday life had led to wide differences of opinion and deep divisions within the church.

Those members who called for reform within the church came to be called Protestants (those who protest). Eventually, the Protestants broke from the Catholic Church entirely. In some European countries, such as Germany, Norway, Sweden, Denmark, and Holland, Protestantism became the official religion, and their rulers closed all Catholic institutions, including most of the hospitals. In England King Henry VIII shut down all the Catholic monasteries, seized all the land and property owned by the church, and banished Catholic clergy from the country. This left most of England without an adequate hospital system. By the mid-1500s, however, the five largest of London's hospitals were handed over to the city government and put back into service.

Rapidly growing populations during the sixteenth and seventeenth centuries led to overcrowded cities, with severe sanitation problems and lots of disease. Without the Catholic monasteries, hospitals, and religious nursing orders, people living in Protestant countries faced a serious lack of adequate health care. The hospitals that were left became filthy, dark, vermin-infested, poorly run places. "The hospitals of cities were like prisons," wrote nursing historians Mary Adelaide Nutting and Lavinia Lloyd Dock, "with bare, undecorated walls and little dark rooms, small windows where no sun could enter, and dismal wards where fifty or one hundred patients were crowded together, deprived of all comforts and even of necessities."[6]

In addition to the awful conditions in the hospitals, there was a severe shortage of nurses available to provide care. Those that were employed had very little motivation to provide good-quality care. They were paid very little. The work of nursing was extremely hard, and nurses worked very long hours, sometimes days at a time. Nurses not only saw to the patients, they also had to cook, clean, and do laundry and many other menial tasks. No "respectable" woman would choose to work as a nurse if she had any other way of earning a living. Nursing care was carried out mostly by untrained, illiterate, inexperienced women, often from the lowest ranks of society, such as alcoholics, prisoners, thieves, and even prostitutes.

Another result of the Reformation was that as monks were removed from care of the sick, men disappeared almost entirely from nursing. The exception was in the management of the hospitals, where men assumed leadership and total control over nursing. This period, beginning in about 1550, is sometimes called the dark period of nursing, and little progress was made in the improvement of nursing care. So it remained until the end of the eighteenth century, when reformers began to work for change and improvement in health care and nursing.

Chapter Two

The Nightingale Revolution

During the time known as the dark period of nursing, from about 1550 until about 1850, very little progress was made in the quality of nursing care. This was especially true in Protestant countries such as England, France, Switzerland, Holland, Germany, and the Scandinavian countries (Sweden, Denmark, and Norway), where the Protestant Reformation had effectively shut down almost all Catholic institutions that provided care. The new, more scientific ways of thinking and learning about medicine that had arisen in Europe during the Renaissance did not carry over into nursing. Nursing was still considered a lowly task, not requiring scientific thought and certainly not considered to be related in any way to the "higher art" of medicine. Change, however, was on the horizon.

A Changing Environment for Nursing

By the sixteenth century, some reform efforts had already been made. In England rules governing who could work as a nurse and how nurses were to behave were developed. Reform efforts also took place within what remained of the Catholic Church in the Protestant countries. One of the most notable was the nursing order called the Sisters of Charity, founded in 1633 in France. Overcrowded cities, almost constant warfare, and lack of quality health care had created an abysmal situation for the ill and poor of Paris, the capital city of France. In response to the need for good-quality, well-managed health care, French priest Vincent de Paul (1576–1660) and noblewoman Louise de Marillac established the Sisters of Charity. Its eleven members, young single women of Paris, visited the sick in their own homes and in Paris hospitals, offering high-quality nursing care and spiritual comfort. The Sisters of Charity order was revolutionary for nursing because it had strict requirements for acceptance into the order, a five-year training program, and distinctive uniforms. The care provided by the sisters was organized, regular, and consistent, and they came to know their patients very well. Soon branches of the order were started in other towns. By 1660, the year both of its founders died, there were more than forty Sisters of Charity houses in France. Over the next two hundred years, the order spread to many other countries, and it is still active today.

Reformers outside the church were also working to improve nursing care at this time. One of the first was Englishman John Howard (1727–1789), who devoted much of his life to examining conditions in prisons, hospitals, and asylums for the mentally ill. His extensive writings about what he saw stressed the need for clean, well-lit, and well-ventilated surroundings for the sick. Elizabeth Gurney Fry (1780–1845) worked in the prisons of London and was especially concerned with the health and welfare of female prisoners and their children. (At this time in England, children had to go with their parents into prison if there were no other relatives to care for them.) Fry established a visiting nurses association called the Institute of Nursing Sisters. In

The Sisters of Charity prepare a meal in the Hospital for the Poor in Beaune, France. The order was established in 1633 and is still active today.

Germany Amalie Sieveking (1794–1859) worked for the benefit of groups of people such as the poor or disabled. She also established a visiting nurses group called the Friends of the Poor. In the United States Dorothea Dix (1802–1887) focused her efforts on care of the mentally ill. Because of her work, more than thirty new psychiatric hospitals were built in the United States. Laws were passed to protect patients, who were often treated like criminals, from cruel and inhumane treatment. These and other humanitarian people gradually brought about significant changes in nursing.

The Beginnings of Modern Nursing

The 1800s marked a transition between the dark period of nursing and the beginnings of new, improved, and more modern ways of thinking about nursing. One of the first changes to take place was the revival of deaconess orders by the Protestant Church. An example of this movement was seen in Germany, with the Deaconess Institute at Kaiserworth. The institute was founded in 1836 by German minister Theodor Fliedner and his wife, Friederike. It began as a haven for released prisoners, but the Fliedners later added a small hospital that included a training program for deaconesses. The women who worked there were not paid, but they were housed and supported by the institute for their entire lives.

Kaiserworth provided compassionate, good quality care of the sick and poor, and its reputation grew. Soon so many women wanted to work there that the institute had to expand its housing to accommodate them all. Its three-year training program included education in bedside nursing, visiting nursing, ethics, and pharmacology (the study of medicines and drugs). The influence of Kaiserworth spread to other countries, including the United States, and Kaiserworth-trained deaconesses worked in many parts of the world. The reforms in nursing begun by Kaiserworth also inspired a brand-new system of modern nursing developed by a British nurse named Florence Nightingale, who revolutionized nursing and brought it into the modern age.

The Nightingale Revolution Begins

Nightingale was born on May 12, 1820, in Florence, Italy, while her wealthy English parents were traveling in Europe. Her father provided her and her sister with a thorough classical education in literature, music, languages, history, philosophy, mathematics, and science. It was a time of great social change and reform in England, and Nightingale was influenced by her parents' interest in social welfare, religious freedom, and ending the slave trade. When Nightingale expressed a desire to become a nurse, her family objected because of the bad reputation of nursing at the time. They wanted her to marry well and raise children like other young women in their social circle. Nightingale, however, believed that God had called her

Nineteenth-Century Medicine

The two centuries following the Renaissance are often called the Age of Enlightenment or Age of Reason. It was a time of great social reform in Europe and America, and it was a time of tremendous advances in medicine. Hospitals became places not only for care of the sick but also for medical education and research. Physicians conducted detailed observations of their patients, built laboratories, and conducted experiments to prove their observations about illness. Englishman Edward Jenner developed vaccination, which saved countless lives from the dreaded disease smallpox. Anatomy gained importance as a science, and diseases of many body systems were described and explained. The cellular structures of plants and animals were discovered. New technologies and inventions such as the thermometer, the stethoscope, blood transfusion, blood pressure measurement, and the electrocardiogram provided new ways to diagnose and treat illness.

One of the most significant advances was the discovery that microscopic organisms such as bacteria could cause disease. Scientists such as Louis Pasteur and Robert Koch developed the germ theory of disease, paving the way for vaccination and treatment for many different diseases such as rabies, tuberculosis, and cholera. The germ theory also revolutionized surgery and childbirth by reducing illness and death from infection. The new anesthetic drugs ether and chloroform also made surgery safer and pain free.

to be a nurse, and she refused to give up that calling. In 1845 she asked to be allowed to work at Salisbury Hospital, where the head physician was a family friend, but her parents refused. She again met resistance when she spent some months teaching poor children at a London school called the Ragged School.

Despite her family's opposition, Nightingale would not give up. During a tour of Europe, she took the opportunity to learn about the conditions inside the hospitals and the care the patients received. In Rome she studied the Catholic sisterhoods, and in Germany she spent two weeks at Kaiserworth, where despite continued protests from her family, she took four months of training. In Paris she studied with Saint Vincent de Paul's Sisters of Charity at the newly built Lariboisière Hospital. This hospital impressed her with its open design, which provided light and fresh air and allowed bad air, or miasmas, which she believed was the cause of disease, to escape.

Nightingale returned to London in 1853 to serve as superintendent of a charity hospital called the Establishment

Florence Nightingale believed God had called her to be a nurse. She studied with the Sisters of Charity in France.

for Gentlewomen During Illness. She worked there for one year and was preparing to begin another job as superintendent at King's College Hospital when England went to war in the Crimea, a peninsula located on the northern coast of the Black Sea in what is today the country of Ukraine.

The Lady with the Lamp

Shortly after the Crimean War began in 1853, the people of England began seeing stories about the war in the *Times* by journalist William Howard Russell.

They read his accounts of the horrific conditions being endured by wounded British soldiers in the Crimea. The death rate from injuries, illnesses, and infections was close to 43 percent. The people of England were outraged that their soldiers were dying in such large numbers due to lack of care in the military hospitals.

In response British secretary of war Sidney Herbert, a close friend of Nightingale's, decided to send a group of female nurses to the Crimea to care for the soldiers. This was a radical idea, because women had never been sent to a war as an official part of the military. There was considerable opposition from military authorities, who felt that this was a man's job, but when Queen Victoria gave her blessing to the project, the criticism stopped. Herbert felt that Nightingale was the best person to be in charge of the group. In a letter asking for her help, he expressed his confidence in her ability to get the job done. He described the difficulties that would be involved in putting together a group of nurses with the physical and emotional strength required for such a difficult task. He also promised her the full support of the British government as well as authority over the nurses and the complete cooperation of the army medical staff. Herbert wrote:

There is but one person in England that I know of who would be capable of organizing and superintending such a scheme. . . . I must not conceal from you that I think upon your decision will depend the ultimate success or failure of the plan. Your own personal qualities, your knowledge and your power of administration, and among greater things your rank and position in society give you advantages in such a work which no other person possesses.[7]

Florence Nightingale walks the wards of the Scutari hospital carrying a lamp and caring for wounded British soldiers during the Crimean War. It was the first time women nurses were officially sent to care for war casualties.

On October 21, 1854, Nightingale left England with thirty-eight other volunteer nurses, bound for the military hospital located at Scutari (in modern-day Istanbul, Turkey). The women had been trained by Nightingale herself and included ten Catholic sisters, eight Anglican sisters, six nurses from Saint John's House (an Anglican sisterhood), and fourteen others from various hospitals. Upon their arrival at Scutari, they discovered that conditions there were every bit as horrible as the news reports had stated. Nursing historian M. Patricia Donahue describes what they found:

> The vast Barrack Hospital, which resembled a hollow square with a tower at each corner, was crowded with four miles of beds. It was designed to accommodate 1700 patients, but between 3000 and 4000 were packed into it. Candles stuck in empty beer bottles lit up endless scenes of human agony. An open sewer that attracted rats and vermin was immediately under the building. There was no water and no soap; there were no towels, few utensils of any sort . . . and putrid [rotten] food. Men lay practically naked or in ragged uniforms clotted with blood. Essential surgical and medical supplies were lacking, and there was no dietary or laundry equipment of any kind. The death rate was 42.7%.[8]

Nightingale had strong opinions about how the hospital should be run.

She did not want to anger the doctors there, however, so her first action was to put her nurses under their direction. Despite her efforts to work with the military personnel, Nightingale met opposition to almost everything she wanted to do. The military authorities resisted taking suggestions and directions from a female civilian who was not under their authority. She also had to deal with complaints from some of her own nurses, who had not realized how difficult the job would be. Nightingale did not tolerate this behavior, and nurses who complained too much were sent back to England and replaced with new nurses. Her determination to do what she thought was right earned her the affectionate title "lady-in-chief."

Even with the difficulties from the military personnel and her nurses, Nightingale was able to get the supplies she needed to transform the hospital into a safe and comforting environment. She obtained new clothing and bedding for the soldiers and established a hospital laundry. She improved their diet and added five kitchens. She provided books, cards, educational classes, and other activities for recovering soldiers

The Crimean War, 1853–1856

The Crimean War, during which Florence Nightingale gained fame for her care of wounded soldiers, was a conflict between Russia and an alliance of France and England. The Ottoman Empire (present-day Turkey) was declining in power, and Russia was attempting to gain control over trade routes in the area using military force. The Turks resisted, but when France and England got involved in trying to prevent Russian control, the Turks backed down and gave in to both sides. Another reason for the conflict was religious—the desire of both the Russian Orthodox Church and the French Roman Catholic Church to control important religious places in the Holy Land. Most of the fighting took place around the Black Sea, especially on the Crimean Peninsula. After several major battles (including the Charge of the Light Brigade, about which a classic poem was written by Alfred, Lord Tennyson), the Russians finally withdrew from the area, and the war ended in the spring of 1856.

One of the unique features of the Crimean War was the use of journalists at the front, who reported on events and conditions there. Englishman William Howard Russell of the *Times* reported almost daily on the terrible living conditions and almost complete lack of medical care for sick and injured British soldiers there. A public outcry followed, prompting secretary of war Sidney Herbert to send Nightingale and her nurses to the Crimea.

and helped them send letters and money home to their families. Her nightly rounds throughout the wards earned her another nickname, "the lady with the lamp." The hard work paid off. In only six months the 42.7 percent mortality rate had dropped to 2.2 percent.

With conditions at Scutari greatly improved, Nightingale traveled across the Black Sea to the Crimean Peninsula and visited two military hospitals there. She went to the front lines of the battle but became ill with a fever and almost died. She recovered but never regained all of her strength. In 1856 she returned to England four months after the end of the war. The rest of her career was spent working to improve nursing education in England and to improve military health care. In her later years her eyesight and hearing failed, and she retired to private life. She died on August 13, 1910, at age ninety.

The Legacy of Florence Nightingale

Nightingale's contributions to the profession of nursing extend far beyond her efforts during the Crimean War. After the war, she worked tirelessly to reform and improve the British system of military health care and published her own thoughts on the subject in her book *Notes on Matters Affecting the Health, Efficiency, and Hospital Administration of the British Army* (1858). The book included detailed statistics and diagrams, including a diagram style she invented called a cockscomb diagram, which illustrated the number of war deaths, by month,

from several different causes. It also included her observations on the poor preparation and inadequate education of the doctors in the Crimea and called for an overhaul of British medical education. Her efforts led to the formation of the Royal Commission on the Health of the Army in 1857, and in 1860 the first British army medical school was built. She was often asked for her advice and opinions when new hospitals were built, both military and civilian.

The work of Nightingale during the Crimean War provided much of the inspiration for the founding of the International Red Cross. During an 1859 visit to Solferino, Italy, Swiss businessman Henri Dunant had the opportunity to witness the suffering of soldiers after a battle between French and Austrian forces, which had taken place the very day he arrived there. He was dismayed to find that only two physicians were available to treat more than six thousand wounded soldiers, so he enlisted local people to provide care for the wounded and sick. He felt that there should be some kind of international organization to see to the care of wounded soldiers in the future, and appealed to several European governments for support of his idea. Much of his arguments for the organization were based on Nightingale's success during the Crimean War. In February 1863 the International Red Cross was officially established.

Nightingale brought to nursing a new and different philosophy. She wrote of two different kinds—"sick" nursing and "health" nursing—and often spoke

The Scutari Hospital in the Crimea is shown here after Nightingale's improvements. In six months' time the hospital's mortality rate dropped from 42.7 percent to 2.2 percent.

more about promoting health than about illness. "[Nursing] has been limited to signify little more than the administration of medicines and the application of poultices," she wrote in her 1859 book *Notes on Nursing—What It Is and What It Is Not*. "It ought to signify the proper use of fresh air, light, warmth, cleanliness, quiet, and the proper selection and administration of diet—all at the least expense of vital power to the patient."[9] Interestingly, she never fully believed in the new germ theory of illness, introduced by scientists such as Louis Pasteur and Robert Koch in the late 1800s. As a miasmatist, she believed that illness was caused by miasmas. Her emphasis on sanitation, therefore, was not an effort to decrease germs, but to eliminate mias-

mas from the patient's environment. "The very first canon of nursing," she wrote, "the first and last thing upon which a nurse's attention must be fixed . . . is this: to keep the air he breathes as pure as the external air, without chilling him."[10]

Nightingale also had a lasting effect on how nurses are educated. She approached nursing education from a scientific point of view and thought of the practice of nursing as separate and distinct from the practice of medicine. She saw nursing education as a systematic, ordered process and understood that sometimes students first had to be taught how to think about education—they had to be taught how to learn. "Observation," she wrote in 1882, "tells *how* the patient is; reflection tells *what* is to be done; training tells *how* it is to be done. Training and experience are, of course, necessary to teach us, too, *how* to observe, *what* to observe; *how* to think, *what* to think."[11]

In 1860 Nightingale established one of the earliest formal training programs for nurses in England, the Florence Nightingale School of Nursing and Midwifery. Students at the school, located at Saint

Mary Seacole

Mary Seacole was a Jamaican nurse who served in the Crimean War and was honored for the care she provided there. She was born in 1805 in Kingston, Jamaica (a British military outpost at the time), the daughter of a free Creole woman and a Scottish soldier. She learned about herbal medicine from her mother and earned a reputation as a skilled healer and nurse to the soldiers in Kingston. In 1851 she traveled to Panama to visit her brother and provided her nursing skills during an outbreak of cholera there. Back in Jamaica she assisted during a yellow fever outbreak.

At the onset of the Crimean War, Seacole went to London and tried multiple times to join the war effort as a nurse, but her offers were repeatedly turned down. She was bitterly disappointed by this. She wrote in her 1857 autobiography that she suspected she was turned down because of her race: "Doubts and suspicions arose in my heart for the first and last time, thank Heaven. Was it possible that American prejudices against colour had some root here? Did these ladies shrink from accepting my aid because my blood flowed beneath a somewhat duskier skin than theirs?" Despite these obstacles, she went to the Crimea on her own, using money she raised herself. Once there she built a hotel out of driftwood and discarded metal, where she sold provisions and pro-

vided meals and nursing services. She often went to the battlefields to tend to wounded soldiers and earned the nickname "the Black Nightingale."

At the end of the war, Seacole was one of the last to leave the Crimea. She spent her remaining years in Jamaica and London. She died in May 1881.

Quoted in Mary Seacole. *Wonderful Adventures of Mrs. Seacole in Many Lands.* London: Blackwood, 1857. www.gutenberg.org/files /23031/23031-h/23031-h.htm.

Jamaican-born Mary Seacole's care for Crimean War casualties earned her the nickname "the Black Nightingale."

Thomas's Hospital in London, learned about home and hospital care, care of the poor, careful record keeping, and teaching patients and their families about health. At first, she faced almost overwhelming opposition to the school from the physicians of London. In a pamphlet called *Facts Relating to Hospital Nurses*, one doctor wrote, "As regards the nurses or ward-maids, these are in much the same position as house-maids, and require little teaching beyond that of poultice-making."[12] Despite this opposition, the school was a success, and its graduates were in high demand in hospitals in England and other countries. Nightingale's school served as a model for other schools of nursing and helped make nursing a respectable and desirable occupation for women. By her death in 1910, there were twenty Nightingale schools throughout Europe, Asia, the Middle East, and North America.

The influence of Nightingale on the nursing profession cannot be overestimated. As medical historian Victor Robinson wrote, "The definite dividing line between the old nursing and the new is the demarcation between pre-Nightingale nursing and Nightingale nursing. In the sense that Hippocrates was the father of medicine Florence Nightingale was the founder of nursing. . . . Miss Nightingale hewed a new profession out of centuries of ignorance and superstition."[13] Today International Nurses Day is celebrated on her birthday. She has been memorialized in dozens of songs and poems. In 1857 Henry Wadsworth Longfellow immortalized Nightingale in his poem "Santa Filomena," which reads in part:

Thus thought I, as by night I read
Of the great army of the dead,
The trenches cold and damp,
The starved and frozen camp,—

The wounded from the battle plain,

In dreary hospitals of pain—

The cheerless corridors,

The cold and stony floors.

Lo! In that house of misery,

A lady with a lamp I see

Pass through the glimmering gloom,

And flit from room to room.

A Lady with a Lamp shall stand
In the great history of the land,
A noble type of good,
Heroic womanhood.[14]

Chapter Three

Nursing Becomes a Profession

A profession is generally defined as a full-time occupation that requires a high level of training and expertise, a code or model for behavior and responsibility, and a certain level of control over its own practice. Florence Nightingale always referred to nursing as a profession, and she helped elevate it out of the dark period by changing the way people viewed nursing, holding nurses to very high standards of competence and behavior, and promoting nursing education through her system of schools. She turned a disrespected occupation into a modern, science-based, respectable, and sought-after occupation for women of the nineteenth century. By the second half of the century, there were two separate classes of nurses—lower-class working nurses, or ward maids, who needed to work for a living; and so-called lady nurses—wealthy, educated women who went into nursing as a charitable pursuit and received formal training. Nursing continued to evolve throughout the nineteenth century in both Europe and America and finally came into its own as a true profession. The evolution began with education.

The Evolution of Nursing Education

At the beginning of the 1800s, there were very few formal nursing education programs in Europe or America except for those provided by Catholic orders, and those were open only to members of the orders. New nurses learned by doing the job, with the occasional lecture from a physician or medical student. By the mid-1800s some efforts were made at improved training for nurses. In 1861 two female physicians, Ann Preston and Emmelin H. Cleveland, opened Women's Hospital of Philadelphia. This institution actually focused more on nursing education than on care of patients. In Boston the New England Hospital for Women and Children, also founded by female doctors and staffed entirely by women, added a six-month training program in 1863. In general, however, education for nurses lacked support, especially from physicians.

In the second half of the nineteenth century, interest in adequate education for nurses increased. At this time, many important advances were being made in medical science and technology, and education for nurses was needed so that they could put this new knowledge into practice on the wards. In America the enormous death rate of soldiers in the Civil War from illness and infection illustrated how inadequate American nursing care was. In England the successes of Nightingale's work in the Crimea and her school at Saint Thomas's Hospital had demonstrated the impact that good nursing care had on the health and well-being of ill and injured people. In a drastic change in attitude from pre-Nightingale days, support for better nursing schools now came from both physicians and the public. In 1868 Samuel D. Gross, president of the American

The women's ward at Middlesex Hospital, London, is shown. Women's hospitals were founded by female doctors, and their staffs focused more on nursing education than on care of patients.

Medical Association (AMA) and one of the most influential physicians of the time, wrote:

> It seems to me to be just as necessary to have well-trained, well-instructed nurses as to have intelligent and skillful physicians. I have long been of the opinion that there ought to be in all the principal towns and cities of the Union institutions for the education of men and women whose duty it is to take care of the sick and to carry out the injunctions [orders] of the medical attendant. It does not matter what may be the skill of the medical practitioner . . . his efforts can be of comparatively little avail unless they are seconded by an intelligent and devoted nurse. Myriads of human beings perish annually in the so-called civilized world for the want of good nursing.[15]

The following year the AMA's Committee on the Training of Nurses issued a document proposing that every large hospital have a nursing school, that physicians should do the teaching, that students should live together in a supervised home, and that county nursing schools not associated with a hospital should also be established.

Support for quality nursing education also came from the public, especially from women of wealthy families who were interested in nursing as a career. An 1871 editorial article called "Lady Nurses" expressed this support in a magazine for women called *Godey's Lady's Book*. The editor of the magazine wrote:

> Much has been lately said of the benefits that would follow if the calling of sick nurse were elevated to a profession which an educated lady might adopt without a sense of degradation. There can be no doubt that the duties of sick nurse, to be properly performed, require an education and training little, if at all, inferior to those possessed by members of the medical profession. . . . Every medical college should have a course of study and training especially adapted for ladies who desire to qualify themselves for the profession of nurse; and those who had gone through the course, and passed the requisite examination, should receive a degree and a diploma, which would at once establish their position in society. The graduate nurse would in general estimation be as much above the ordinary nurse of the present day as the professional surgeon of our time is above the barber-surgeon of the last century.[16]

America's First Trained Nurses

In 1872 the New England Hospital for Women and Children admitted five students to its new twelve-month certificate program for nurses. In September 1873 one student graduated. With her nursing certificate in hand, Linda Richards became known as America's first formally trained professional nurse. Then in 1879 Mary Eliza Mahoney completed the program, which had by then expanded to sixteen months, and became the first African American nursing professional. At this time, very few nursing programs admitted African American students, so separate schools were created. The first was Spelman Seminary in Atlanta, Georgia, in 1886. In 1891 Hampton Institute in Virginia and Provident Hospital in Chicago were established to provide nursing education for African American students.

By the time Richards graduated, the Nightingale philosophy of nursing education had come to America. Three Nightingale schools were begun in 1873. The Bellevue Training School in New York City was modeled after the program at Saint Thomas's in London. The program lasted one year, and students were expected to work at the hospital for at least a year after graduation. They were paid ten dollars per month, even during their training, and were the first American nurses to wear uniforms. The director of the program, Helen Bowden, was very familiar with the Nightingale philosophy, and the Nightingale System became known in America as the Bellevue System.

The Connecticut Training School in New Haven was established by Georgeanna Bacon, who had served as a nurse during the Civil War. This school produced one of the first nursing textbooks, the *New Haven Manual of Nursing*. In 1924 the school became affiliated with Yale University, and its nursing program became the first to become a separate university department.

The Boston Training School was established at Massachusetts General Hospital. The school was resisted by the physicians there, and at first it was not run very well. The next year Richards was put in charge, and under her leadership the school became very successful. These three American Nightingale schools served as examples of what nursing education could be, and interest in formal nursing education expanded rapidly. Trained nurses were not only accepted but demanded by hospitals, physicians, and the public. By the end of the century, there were more than four hundred formal training programs for nurses in the United States.

Nurses Become Organized

As the demand for well-trained nurses in hospitals and communities skyrocketed, nursing leaders realized that the profession could be advanced and improved even more if nurses organized themselves on a national level. Organization would allow nurses to set common standards of education and practice nationwide in order to protect the public from poorly trained or untrained caregivers. It would also improve the social status of nurses and nursing and help the profession gain recognition from state and national governments.

The first nursing organization was the British Nurses' Association, founded in 1887 by Bedford and Ethel Fenwick. Ethel was a nurse who had served as matron (a nurse supervisor) of Saint

Linda Richards, America's First Trained Nurse

Melinda Ann Judson Richards, also called Linda, was born near Potsdam, New York, on July 27, 1841. Her father was a traveling preacher, and much of her childhood was spent moving from place to place. When she was four years old, her father died from tuberculosis. Richards's mother moved the family to Vermont, where she also became ill with tuberculosis. Richards nursed her mother until she died. After her mother's death, Richards decided to pursue a career in nursing and was taught by the family doctor who had cared for her mother.

In 1860 she became engaged to George Poole, but before they could be married, he left to fight in the Civil War. In 1865 George was wounded and returned home, and Richards cared for him until he died in 1869. After his death Richards moved to Boston and worked as an assistant nurse at Boston City Hospital. Several months later she heard of the nurses' training program being offered at the New England Hospital for Women and Children. Richards was one of five girls who signed up for the program. After a year of training, Richards became the first graduate of the program. She became the night supervisor at Bellevue Hospital in New York City, one of the first Nightingale schools in the United States. While there she developed a system for creating detailed medical records for each patient, one of the earliest such systems. In 1874 she returned to Boston to supervise the training program there and turned it into one of the best in the country. Three years later she went to London, met Nightingale, and visited her training program at Saint Thomas's Hospital.

From 1886 to 1891 Richards served as a missionary in Japan and opened Japan's first nursing school. After returning to the United States, she opened several more schools and held several other positions with various hospitals and nursing organizations. In 1923 she suffered a stroke and lived the remainder of her life at the New England Hospital for Women and Children. She died on April 16, 1930.

Linda Richards became the first trained American nurse after graduating from the New England Hospital for Women and Children in 1870.

Bartholomew's Hospital in London. After she married Bedford, she retired from practice and devoted her time to working for nursing organization. The Fenwicks brought together a group of physicians and hospital matrons and drafted a charter—a document describing the purposes and goals of the association. One of the association's main goals was to establish registration of nurses, similar to today's licensing of nurses,

Ethel Fenwick, along with her husband, Bedford, founded the British Nurses' Association in 1887. The association established registration of nurses to ensure that nurses were well trained.

which would ensure that nurses were well trained and competent to provide care to patients. Registration would also mean that only those who were properly trained could call themselves nurses.

The idea of registering nurses was not well accepted at first by hospitals and doctors, and even Nightingale opposed the idea. She and others felt that registering nurses would diminish the view of nursing as a compassionate art with a higher calling and make it too technical and too much like medical practice. Despite this resistance, however, the association grew rapidly, reaching one thousand members by the end of its first year. In 1892 it received a royal charter, which gave it official recognition by the Crown, and was renamed the Royal British Nurses' Association.

In America at the 1893 World's Fair in Chicago, nursing leaders made presentations on nursing issues at a meeting of the International Congress of Charities, Corrections, and Philanthropy. A letter from Nightingale about nursing education was read. The next day a group of nursing leaders and nursing school directors from the United States and Canada met to discuss the possibility of establishing an American nursing organization. After the Canadian members left to form their own organization, the American group became known as the National League of Nursing Education. Today it is called the National League for Nursing.

In 1911 one of the largest and most influential American nursing organizations got its start—the American Nurses

Nursing Uniforms

Prior to the nineteenth century, most nursing was done by members of religious orders of nuns. The traditional nun's habit eventually became associated with nursing work and influenced the appearance of early nursing uniforms. With the reforms in nursing begun after the Protestant Reformation, members of secular (non-religious) nursing orders began to wear distinctive uniforms that resembled the nun's habit but still distinguished their members from religious nursing orders. One of the first orders to provide distinctive dress for its members was Saint Vincent de Paul's Sisters of Charity. The sisters wore a gray-blue gown and white apron made of wool, with a starched white collar and a large white headdress called a cornette, which resembled the headdresses worn by nuns. In the early 1800s nurses at the Deaconess Institute at Kaiserworth, Germany, wore a blue cotton gown with a white apron and collar and a white cap that tied under the chin. Students in Nightingale training programs wore a similar uniform, designed by one of the students, with long sleeves, white aprons, collars, and cuffs, and a cap with frills around the face.

As the nursing profession gained respectability after Florence Nightingale's time, hospitals and nursing schools began to design their own uniforms that would give their nurses a professional appearance and distinguish them from nurses of other institutions. Caps especially became unique to each institution, with many variations in style and color. Color was used symbolically—white for cleanliness, blue for purity, etc. Few changes were made in nursing uniforms until the 1940s, when they were shortened in accordance with changing styles in women's clothing. Uniforms usually consisted of a knee-length or midcalf-length white dress, with white stockings, shoes, and cap. As more men entered the profession, pants with tunic tops became popular, even among women. The white uniform remains the standard in many countries today.

In the United States beginning in the 1990s, the traditional white uniform began to be replaced with more practical scrubs, the clothing worn by surgical personnel in the operating room, and caps are rarely worn. Scrubs come in many colors and designs that are often used to distinguish workers from those in other hospital departments.

Association (ANA). It was created to help unify nurses in the forty-six states that existed in 1911. Other goals included ensuring quality health care for patients and influencing government legislation about nursing, especially licensing laws.

Today there are chapters of the ANA in every state.

The first international nursing organization was the International Council of Nurses (ICN), founded in 1899. Its first president was Ethel Fenwick, and the first member nations were the United States, Great Britain, and Germany. Its main purpose was to demonstrate that nurses from many countries had similar goals and ideas about excellence in education and patient care, as well as about the advancement of the nursing profession. Today the ICN has more than 130 member nations and represents more than 13 million nurses around the world. The ANA is the American member organization of the ICN.

Licensure and Registration

Registration that would separate trained nurses from untrained or poorly trained caregivers was central to getting nursing officially recognized as a true profession. The first recorded mention of nursing licensure came in 1860 from physician Henry W. Acland of Oxford University Hospital in Oxford, England. Unlike most physicians of his time, he felt strongly that nurses should have standards for education, be registered with the government, and meet minimum standards of competence. In 1919, after thirty years of effort, the Royal British Nurses' Association finally succeeded in getting licensure for nurses in England.

In the United States, American nurses pressed for licensing laws that would

Registered nurses of St. Mark's Hospital in New York City pose for a photo circa 1906. In 1903, New York, North Carolina, New Jersey, and Virginia became the first states to pass nurse licensing laws.

distinguish properly trained nursing school graduates from others. The responsibility for licensing nurses fell to the states rather than to the federal government, so state nursing organizations were established to accomplish this task. In 1903 four states—North Carolina, New Jersey, New York, and Virginia—passed licensure laws.

Nurses Begin to Specialize

Before the twentieth century hospitalized patients were usually put into general wards, with no separation according to their diagnosis. In some of the worst hospitals, patients with infectious, or spreadable, diseases might even be put into the same bed with each other or into beds with patients who had just had surgery. Nurses were expected to care for all patients regardless of the reason they were in the hospital.

After the innovations made by Nightingale and others, this practice stopped. Patients were now separated into wards by diagnosis. Nurses working in a particular ward became very skilled at taking care of the health issues of the patients in that ward. In this way nurses began to specialize.

Nurse-Midwives

Some specialization among nurses had already existed for some time. For example, the nurse-midwife had existed for centuries, tending to pregnant women during and after childbirth. Throughout most of human history, this task had been done almost exclusively by women. In the nineteenth century, however, with advances in medicine and the growth of medical schools, childbirth increasingly became attended more by physicians than midwives. Conflicts over who was best suited to fill this role arose between physicians and midwives. Most wealthier women preferred to have a physician, but untrained midwives still tended to poorer women and those living in rural areas. Normal deliveries were usually carried out successfully, but if the birth was complicated, there was a high chance of death for the mother, the baby, or both. The need for trained midwives became apparent. In 1832 Joseph Warrington began providing some training for midwives at his hospital in Philadelphia. In Boston Samuel Gregory did the same in 1846. In 1911 Belleview Hospital in New York City opened a school of midwifery.

In 1925, in response to the high rate of maternal and newborn deaths among poor and rural patients, Mary Breckinridge founded the Frontier Nursing Service to serve the people in the hills of Kentucky, who until then had relied on the services of illiterate "grannies." Breckinridge wrote, "To meet the needs of the frontiersman's child, you must begin before he is born and carry him through the hazards of childbirth. This means that the nurses who serve him must be qualified as midwives. They must be nurse-midwives."[17]

Because there were so few formally trained midwives in the nation at the time, Breckinridge brought trained nurse-midwives to the United States from England. She divided the area to

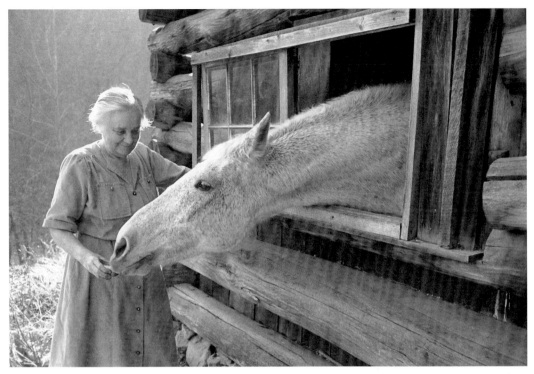

Mary Breckinridge, nurse and midwife, founded the Frontier Nursing Service in 1925 in rural Kentucky to better meet the needs of frontier mothers and babies.

be served into eight districts of 78 square miles (202 sq km) each, with two nurses providing care for all the women living within their district. If a delivery became complicated, the midwife would send for a physician to help. The nurses also provided child-care services and education on child rearing to parents. Breckinridge wrote:

> Even after his birth the young child is not an isolated individual. His care not only means the care of his mother before, during and after his birth, but the care of his whole family as well. Bedside nursing of the sick in their homes is as essential in rural areas as in the Visiting Nurse Associations of cities. It means including the whole family, because the young child is part of his family. Health teaching must also be on a family basis—in the homes.[18]

In 1935 a small hospital was built to provide better services, and in 1939 the Frontier Nursing Service founded the Graduate School of Midwifery.

Public Health Nursing

Another traditional specialty role for early nurses was that of public health nursing. The general concept had begun with Nightingale in England. In the United States Breckinridge's Frontier Nursing Service provided public health nursing as well as midwife services. In the early twentieth century, visiting nurse associations appeared in cities such as Boston, New York, Chicago, and Philadelphia, sending nurses wherever they were needed. Some public health nurses cared for poor urban people who could not afford a physician, visiting them in their own homes. Others cared for those who lived in isolated rural areas who could not get to a city for hospital care.

Public health nurses provided a wide array of nursing services, from giving medicines to setting broken bones and delivering babies. Education was also

The Victorian Order of Nurses and the Klondike Expedition

In February 1897 the Victorian Order of Nurses (VON) was established in Canada to provide public health nurses for people in remote areas of the country. One of its first missions, and one of its most dangerous, was to send four well-trained nurses to the Klondike, a remote and very rugged subarctic area of the Yukon Territory of Canada, to treat people who had gone there for the Canadian gold rush. The traveling was very difficult—on horseback or on foot, over terrain that was sometimes rocky and steep, sometimes low and swampy. "Those devoted women," wrote Ishbel Aberdeen to a Canadian newspaper, "fear not to face the perils and privations which their mission must necessarily impose on them. On the contrary, they rejoice at such an opportunity being afforded so soon to the Victorian Order to show what nurses may do for suffering humanity under such adverse circumstances."

When the nurses arrived at the boomtown of Dawson, they found an epidemic of typhoid fever raging. Overcrowding, bad food and water, and poor sanitation created perfect conditions for typhoid. The death rate was more than two hundred on some days. Some of the men had other illnesses as well, such as pneumonia, malaria, and scurvy (severe vitamin C deficiency); others needed treatment for injuries. Conditions for the nurses were bad, too, with limited food and supplies, little communication with the outside world, sparse accommodations, and bitterly cold weather. Still, the nurses went out into the wilderness to look for men who had become ill and bring them back to the small hospital in the town.

By 1900 the epidemic and the gold rush had subsided. The work of the four VON nurses in the Klondike received praise from the Canadian government, the military, the church, and the public.

Ishbel Aberdeen, letter to the editor, *Quebec Saturday Budget*, March 12, 1898. http://news.google.com/newspapers?nid=450&dat=18980312&id=0hlMAAAAIBAJ&sjid=Uy4DAAAAIBAJ&pg=536 8,3140416.

an important job for these nurses. They taught families about child care, nutrition and food preparation, hygiene, sanitation, and disease prevention and recovery. They also worked in factories and mines, seeing to the welfare of the workers, and provided care for children in school.

Public health nursing was not an easy job. Early in the century there was a severe shortage of public health nurses, so they worked long hours each day. Because their patients were poor, they often received no pay. Rural health nurses often had to travel many miles to reach all of their patients regularly. If there were no roads, they traveled on mules, on horseback, or on foot, carrying their packs of supplies with them. One nurse was known for arriving at her patients' homes on a motorcycle. Visiting nurses who worked in overcrowded, filthy city slums were exposed to diseases such as typhoid and tuberculosis, and they risked danger in unsafe neighborhoods. Many of their patients were new immigrants from Europe, so nurses often had to manage cultural and language barriers.

Lillian Wald and the Henry Street Settlement

One of the earliest and most influential pioneers in public health nursing was Lillian Wald (1867–1940). She is credited with coining the prase "public health nurse" in 1893. Born into a wealthy family, Wald was educated at upscale schools for young ladies. She graduated from the New York Hospital Training School

for Nurses in 1891 and soon became aware of the need for health care and other social services for the poor. After a year of nursing, she entered medical school at the Women's Medical College in New York. During that time, she was assigned to go into the city's Lower East Side, an area of poor, mostly immigrant families, to teach mothers there about caring for the sick.

One day while Wald was giving a class on bed making in an old building on Henry Street, a little girl approached her and asked for help for her sick mother, who had given birth two days earlier. Wald wrote:

The child led me over broken roadways, over dirty mattresses and heaps of refuse . . . between tall, reeking houses . . . past odorous fish stands, for the streets were a marketplace, unregulated, unsupervised, unclean; past evil-smelling, uncovered garbage cans. . . . The child led me on through a tenement hallway . . . up into a rear tenement, by slimy steps whose accumulated dirt was augmented that day by the mud of the streets, and finally into the sickroom. . . . The sick woman lay on a wretched, unclean bed, soiled with a hemorrhage two days old.[19]

With that experience, Wald decided to leave the college and devote herself to living and working in the Lower East Side. With the help of a wealthy friend, she bought the Henry Street building

Lillian Wald was an early pioneer in public health nursing. She established the Henry Street Settlement in New York City to provide health care and nursing services, social services, and educational and cultural activities for those in need.

and established the Henry Street Visiting Nurse Service, or Henry Street Settlement, in 1895. The settlement provided health care and nursing services, along with social services, education, and cultural activities. Other nursing settlements soon appeared in other cities, following the Henry Street model. Over the next several years, the Henry Street Settlement added more buildings, a gymnasium, a playground, a theater, a music school, a school nurse, and summer camps for children.

Surgical Nursing and Nurse Anesthesia

Two other opportunities for nursing specialization arose in the operating room. One of the most important medical advances of the late eighteenth century was the discovery that microscopic organisms could cause disease. The "germ theory," described by Louis Pasteur and Robert Koch, revolutionized surgery by providing the means to prevent and control surgical infections. With this knowledge, surgeons added two important concepts to their practice: antisepsis, the use of chemicals to kill germs; and asepsis, a variety of measures taken to keep the surgical environment as germ free as possible. Maintaining cleanliness, hygiene, and sanitation was already a major responsibility of the nurse, but now there was a much clearer understanding of why it was so important. In a nursing textbook from the late 1800s, author Rachel Norris wrote, "Antiseptic Surgery is based upon the theory that putrefaction [breakdown of flesh] is due to the presence of microscopic germs in the air, in water, on the clothes, or on the hands, in fact, upon everything that is not in itself antiseptic. It is thought that putrefaction is, perhaps, the greatest cause of mischief in open wounds."[20]

In the 1840s another major advance was made in surgery—the discovery of relatively safe and effective anesthetics. Ether and, later, chloroform were early anesthetic chemicals that not only made surgery painless for the patient, but allowed the surgeon to slow down and take more care with the procedure.

With these two major advances, surgery became much more common, and nurses began to specialize in the pre- and postoperative care of the surgical patient. Nurses also began to participate during the surgery itself, as assistants to the surgeon. Nurses who became skilled at administering anesthesia became nurse anesthetists, another new opportunity for specialization.

Nursing Looks to the Twentieth Century

With the establishment of formal standards for education and practice, the formation of nursing organizations, the passage of licensure laws for nurses, and specialization, nursing had finally become a true profession. As nursing leader Mary Adelaide Nutting (1858–1948) wrote in 1905:

We claim, and I think justly, the status of a profession. We have schools and teachers, tuition fees and scholarships, systems of instruction from preparatory to postgraduate; we are allied with technical schools on one hand and here and there a university on the other; we have libraries, a literature, and fast-growing numbers of periodicals owned, edited, and published by nurses; we have societies and laws. If therefore we claim to receive the appurtenances, privileges, and standing of a profession, we must recognize professional responsibilities and obligations which we are honor bound to respect and uphold.[21]

The nineteenth century brought significant changes in nursing. "Those who nursed the sick," writes physician Christine Hallett, "had been transformed . . . from a downtrodden, poorly paid, and reviled group of outcasts, to a highly respected profession whose members had a clear sense of their place in society. The scene was set for the further development of their profession in the turbulent twentieth century."[22]

Chapter Four

Nurses at War

Many of the most important advances in medicine and nursing have come from lessons learned during wartime. Because of the nature of war—the numbers and severity of wounds, the changing nature of war injuries as new weapons are developed, the kinds of illnesses seen in different war zones—nurses who serve during wars are called upon to learn new skills and adapt to difficult and often dangerous situations.

Nurses are not drafted. They do not have to go to war—they choose to—and they have been choosing to since the beginning of nursing. Nurses such as Florence Nightingale, Clara Barton, and Dorothea Dix transformed nursing because of their contributions during wartime. The value of the nurse at war—to patient, profession, and country—is almost immeasurable.

The American Civil War (1861–1865)

The American Civil War caused more loss of life than any other American war. More than 620,000 people died during this war. Battle wounds, however, accounted for only about one-third of all deaths. The rest, more than four hundred thousand, were caused by disease. In the overcrowded camps in which the soldiers lived, diseases such as measles, whooping cough, mumps, and chicken pox spread rapidly. Mosquito infestations caused widespread outbreaks of malaria. Contaminated food caused typhoid fever, the single leading cause of death from illness. Latrines were often set up near streams, which contaminated the drinking water with human waste and caused intestinal disorders such as dysentery and diarrhea. Poor diet and exposure to bad weather led to malnutrition and deaths from pneumonia.

Wounded soldiers were taken to field "hospitals," which were little more than open tents set up behind the battle lines. Medicines and supplies were always scarce, especially in the Southern states. Antisepsis was not yet known, and overworked, poorly trained, or untrained surgeons treated wounds and amputated limbs, sometimes without washing their hands for several days. Thousands of soldiers died from overwhelming infections after such surgery.

Medical facilities of the time were inadequate to handle the sheer numbers of sick and wounded soldiers. Temporary hospitals were set up in churches, schools, warehouses, hotels, and private homes. Even the Capitol building in Washington, D.C., served as a temporary hospital. The need for improvement was clear.

The U.S. Sanitary Commission

The need for good nursing care became obvious soon after the start of battle. The earliest to volunteer for nursing service were the sisters of various religious orders, such as the American branch of the Sisters of Charity. As the war went on, many more women volunteered their services, some experienced and some not.

Union soldiers lie wounded and awaiting treatment at a Union field hospital in 1861. Field hospitals were little more than open tents where thousands of soldiers were treated with inadequate medicines and supplies by poorly trained and overworked staffs.

Nursing in the American Revolution (1775–1783)

Although there were no trained professional nurses during the American Revolution, the need for nursing care was recognized. Early in the war, the Continental Congress created the Hospital of the Army. Doctors who worked for the military were very poorly paid and undersupplied. Care of wounded soldiers in overcrowded, filthy battlefield "hospitals" was deplorable. Care in community hospitals was little better. In both settings thousands died from wound infections and from diseases such as smallpox, scurvy, typhoid, and dysentery.

The great majority of the care of sick and wounded soldiers was carried out by other soldiers. Still, the need for female nurses in the hospitals was felt. In June 1775 Major General Horatio Gates reported to George Washington that "the sick suffered much for want of good female nurses."[1] In response, Washington called for Congress to budget for one hospital nurse for every ten patients, and one supervising matron for every one hundred patients. First aid and nursing care were also provided in private homes near the battlefields by housewives, servants, slaves, and even midwives. Other nurses served in military prisons. Soldiers who were fortunate enough to be near religious houses or churches when they got sick or wounded received quality care from nuns and monks. Some wives of soldiers and officers, including Martha Washington, accompanied their husbands to the field to help care for the men of the regiment. One, Mary Slocumb, described her experience during the Battle of Moore's Creek Bridge. Just after treating a wounded soldier in the field, an officer approached her, as she explained:

> While I was busy Caswell came up. He appeared very much surprised to see me. . . . "Pray," said he, "how came you here?" "O, I thought," replied I, "you would need nurses as well as soldiers. See! I have already dressed many of these good fellows; and here is one"—going to Frank and lifting him up with my arm under his head so he could drink some more water—"would have died before any of you men could have helped him."[2]

1. Quoted in Women in the U.S. Army. "The Army Nurse Corps." www.army.mil/women/nurses.html.
2. Quoted in John Clement, ed. *Noble Deeds of American Women: With Biographical Sketches of Some of the More Prominent.* Williamstown, MA: Corner House, 1975, p. 327.

Some were women from wealthy families who felt a calling to help in the war effort. Many were the wives of soldiers, who accompanied their husbands to war and even fought in battle alongside them.

Volunteer nurses had a significant impact on the care the soldiers received, but there was a need to organize such volunteer efforts. In 1861 the U.S. Sanitary Commission was established. The job of the commission was to investigate the conditions under which Union soldiers were being cared for in field camps and hospitals, collect and distribute supplies, and make sure that doctors were competent and hospitals were kept sanitary. The commission also made sure that the soldiers were kept clean, had enough food and drinkable water, and were not overcrowded.

The commission sent nurses wherever they were needed the most. Dorothea Dix, a nurse who had distinguished herself with her work to improve care for the mentally ill, was appointed superintendent of female nurses for the army. The nurses prepared for their jobs at major hospitals such as Bellevue in New York and several others in Boston. "Women from all parts of the country offered their service," writes nursing historian Minnie Goodnow. "Miss Dix gave preference to middle-aged [those between thirty-five and fifty] and plain featured–women [because she felt they would be less likely to be a distraction for the soldiers]. Some who she refused applied direct to the Secretary of War, and were accepted. Many young women went with their husbands' regiments, and proved so useful that they were allowed to remain. Over two thousand lay women served as nurses during the four years of the war."[23] In addition, according to Goodnow, "many men, ex-patients, orderlies, men unfit for active service, etc., were nurses all during the war. Public opinion was still inclined to the doctrine that men should care for men."[24]

By the end of the nineteenth century, wars had brought the necessity for good nursing care into sharp focus. In 1898, following the Spanish-American War, American Red Cross (ARC) president and nurse Clara Barton made the ARC's nursing services available to the American military. In 1901 the Army Reorganization Bill provided for a permanent Army Nurse Corps that would be part of the army's medical department. Its motto was "Where go the United States troops, there go the Army nurses." In 1908 the U.S. Navy Nurse Corps became a permanent part of the American navy.

Nurses in World War I (1914–1918)

The twentieth century was only fourteen years old when, on June 28, 1914, Archduke Franz Ferdinand of Austria was assassinated while in Sarajevo, Serbia. The assassination led Austria to declare war on Serbia. A chain reaction of declarations of war involving complex treaties between many nations followed, and within months the world was at war. At its height 135 nations were involved in the war at some level. After a long struggle to remain neutral, the United States finally entered the war in April 1917.

World War I (WWI) created a huge demand for doctors, nurses, and other medical personnel. New weapons and combat tactics, such as the machine gun, trench warfare, and submarine and aerial attacks, created large numbers of very severe injuries. Toxic gases such as chlorine, phosgene, tear gas, and mustard

Clara Barton

One of the best-known Civil War nurses was Clara Barton (1821–1912). Barton was a Massachusetts schoolteacher who had received a government job in Washington but was dismissed for her outspoken views on slavery and social justice. When the Civil War broke out, she tended to wounded soldiers in the temporary hospital in the Capitol. She organized her own relief effort, separate from the Sanitary Commission, and saw to the delivery of large amounts of medical supplies, clothing, food, and other supplies to army hospitals. She served as a nurse in the hospitals and on the battlefield, caring for both black and white soldiers from both the North and the South. During one battle, a bullet went through her sleeve and killed the soldier she was tending. After the war she established the Office of Missing Soldiers to try to locate more than

eighty thousand missing men. She worked with suffragist Susan B. Anthony for women's rights and with abolitionist Frederick Douglass for black civil rights. During a four-year stay in Europe, she learned about the Red Cross, and she served as a Red Cross nurse during the Franco-Prussian War (1870–1871). She was so impressed with the Red Cross that when she returned to the United States, she worked to establish the American Red Cross in 1881, and she served as its first president for twenty-three years. She died from tuberculosis at age ninety.

Clara Barton established the American Red Cross in 1881 and served as its first president.

gas caused blindness, confusion, damage to the throat and lungs, blistering of the skin, and often death.

Adding to the massive battlefield casualties was a pandemic, or worldwide outbreak, of a deadly strain of influenza. It began in 1918 in the United States and spread with the movement of troops to all parts of the world. By the time the pandemic subsided in 1920, it had infected almost 30 percent of the world's population. It killed between 50 million and 100 million people around the globe. Even U.S. president Woodrow Wilson became ill, but he recovered. The flu epidemic further stretched medical resources because doctors and nurses were needed to treat the sick; many became ill or died from the flu themselves.

A severe shortage of nurses developed very quickly in Europe. Even before the United States officially entered the war, the U.S. Army and Navy Nurse Corps and the ARC provided nurses for the war effort. After the United States entered the war in 1917, the ARC recruited almost twenty-four thousand more nurses for the army and navy. To help meet the need for nurses both at home and overseas, the National Committee on Emergency Nursing was appointed by the federal government. The committee's major task was to recruit as many new students into nursing schools as possible. Nursing schools increased their facilities, added more teachers, shortened working hours, and relaxed requirements for admission and graduation. In May 1918 the government provided funding for the Army School of Nursing, which provided training at no cost to students. Enrollment in nursing schools rose sharply.

Frontline Nursing in World War I

The American military hospital service in WWI was divided into four stages. Wounded soldiers were first taken to dressing stations, located very near the battlefield, for emergency first aid. They were then sent to field hospitals a little further back. The next stop was the evacuation hospital (the evac), about 10 miles

A U.S. school gymnasium is converted into a flu ward that features beds separated by screens and masked health-care workers. The 1918 flu pandemic caused the death of five hundred thousand Americans and millions worldwide.

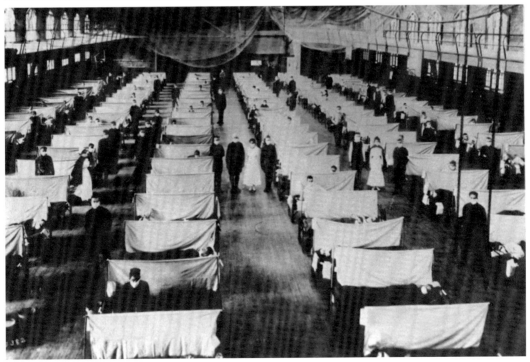

(16km) from the front. Eventually, those who survived were sent to base hospitals for recovery. Nurses did not serve in the dressing stations, and only very rarely in the field hospitals, but provided almost all care given in the evacs and the base hospitals.

Nurses serving in WWI hospitals were challenged to respond to huge numbers of sick and wounded soldiers with life-threatening conditions such as blood loss, wound infections, gas inhalation, and influenza and other infectious diseases. Ellen N. LaMotte, an American nurse who served in a French field hospital, wrote:

This is how it was. It is pretty much always like this in a field hospital. Just ambulances rolling in, and dirty, dying men, and the guns off there in the distance! Very monotonous, and the same, day after day, till one gets so tired and bored. . . . The weariness of it—the sameness of it! The same ambulances, and dirty men, and groans, or silence. The same hot operating rooms, the same beds, always full, in the wards. This is war. But it goes on and on, over and over, day after day, till it seems like life.[25]

One nurse from Utah was "attached to Evacuation Hospital No. 1. In one night alone more than 800 wounded American soldiers were brought into this hospital, 136 of whom were assigned to her care for want of sufficient nurses."[26] Because of the overwhelming numbers of casualties, the severity of their injuries, and the shortage of medical personnel, nurses learned to act independently of physicians and make their own decisions about care.

Of the almost twenty-four thousand American nurses who served during World War I, 296 died in the line of duty in America and Europe, two-thirds of them from pneumonia and influenza. After the war many nurses received awards from the U.S. and foreign governments. One navy nurse, Lenah S. Higbee, even had a new destroyer named for her, the first time a battleship had been named for a woman. In 1920, with the help of the movement for women's voting rights, army nurses were granted official rank, including officer status, by the U.S. Congress.

World War I ended in 1918, but this did not mean that the world was at peace. Political instability in Europe and Asia, combined with a worldwide economic depression beginning in 1929, created conditions ripe for hostility. Ten years later, the world was once again at war.

World War II

The twenty years following WWI was a time of continued political instability in Europe, for a variety of complex reasons. Germany in particular was very dissatisfied with the terms of the treaty that had ended the war. In 1939 German chancellor Adolf Hitler invaded the nations of Czechoslovakia and Poland, sparking declarations of war from Great Britain and France. In 1941 Germany staged a surprise attack on its own ally, the Soviet Union, which drew it into the war as well.

The United States had no desire to get involved in another war, but when Japan, an ally of Germany, attacked the United States by bombing its naval base at Pearl Harbor, Hawaii, in December 1941, the United States declared war on Japan. Two days later Japan's allies Italy and Germany declared war on the United States. Once again, America was at war, and once again, America's nurses geared up to meet the challenge.

The U.S. Cadet Nurse Corps

In 1941 the U.S. government provided $1.2 million for the training of new nurses for national defense. The next year the amount was raised to $3.5 million. In 1943 the Bolton Act, introduced by Representative Frances Payne Bolton, provided $60 million for the creation of the U.S. Cadet Nurse Corps. Students in the corps received a thirty-month program in an approved nursing school, free tuition, textbooks, uniforms, and a monthly allowance. In return they agreed to serve wherever they were needed for the duration of the war and for six months after.

More than eleven hundred nursing schools participated in the program. In order to receive funding from the Bolton Act, participating schools had to meet strict standards of quality and were required to accept all qualified applicants with no discrimination because of race or religion. More than 124,000 new nurses graduated from the pro-

gram. Julia C. Stimson, president of the ANA, cautioned the new nurses, "War is three-quarters waiting and boredom and tiresomeness, and it is one quarter the hardest work you have ever heard of in your life or ever dreamed of."[27]

Nursing at the Front

World War II (WWII) had several major differences from WWI that affected nurses directly. Advances in weaponry, such as automatic rifles, antitank weapons, flamethrowers, and hand grenades, led to higher numbers of casualties and even more severe kinds of wounds than had been seen in WWI. During WWII nurses had to learn to cope emotionally with

A poster recruits women for the U.S. Cadet Nurse Corps during World War II. The corps trained 124,000 new nurses.

the injuries caused by these weapons and treat them appropriately. Another major difference was that, more than in any other war before, attacks on civilian populations were common and caused widespread death and injury in the towns and cities of Europe. For example, during the Blitz of 1940, the German air force bombed London, England, for fifty-seven nights in a row, then bombed many other towns across England and Ireland. More than forty thousand civilians were killed during the eight-month Blitz. Nurses caring for injured citizens found themselves in danger of having their hospitals bombed and having to travel through the cities at night with no light during forced blackouts.

Nurses in other areas of the world dealt with similar dangers. Nurses participated in the 1944 D-day invasion of the French coast—on hospital ships in the English Channel, tending to the wounded onshore and in field hospitals, and on transport planes taking the wounded back to England. Many nurses working on hospital ships in the Mediterranean Sea and the Pacific Ocean lost their lives when their ships were torpedoed. On the island of Malta, nurses took refuge with civilians in caves and underground granaries while the island was bombed.

In the Far East, nurses were captured and imprisoned when Japanese forces invaded several Pacific island nations. Eleven navy nurses were held in a Japanese prison camp for thirty-seven months. Even in prison, nurses continued to provide care to fellow prisoners.

Many nurses died in the prison camps from malaria, typhoid, dysentery, and malnutrition. Twenty-two Australian nurses who had survived the sinking of their ship were captured on the shore of Bangka Island in Indonesia, then forced into the water and shot. Only one survived.

The influence of nursing care in saving lives during WWII cannot be overestimated. Nursing historian M. Patricia Donahue writes:

> The peak strength of the Army and Navy Nurse Corps was nearly 69,000 during World War II. These nurses gave care in front line situations, field hospitals, evacuation hospitals, base hospitals, hospital ships and trains, and in the air. Army nurses served at 9 stations and 52 areas. Navy nurses served on 12 hospital ships and in more than 300 naval stations. Both served wherever the American soldier could be found. More than 1600 nurses were decorated for meritorious service and bravery under fire. . . . A total of 201 [American] nurses died; 16 of these deaths were the result of enemy action.[28]

World War II finally came to an end with the surrender of Japanese and German forces in 1945. In 1949 the Air Force Nurse Corps was established. Only one year later, army, navy, and air force nurses prepared to serve in the next major American war, this time in East Asia.

The Korean War (1950–1953)

One of the conditions for Japanese surrender after WWII was that Japan had to hand over the peninsula of Korea, which Japan had ruled, to American and Soviet control. The peninsula was divided in half, with American forces controlling the southern half and the Soviet Union controlling the northern half. Since the Soviet Union had a communist form of government, North Korea also became a communist nation.

As relations worsened between communist governments, such as Russia and China, and Western capitalist governments, such as the United States and Great Britain, hostilities broke out between North and South Korea. In June 1950 North Korean military forces invaded South Korea. The United States and twenty other nations responded by sending military forces to defend South Korea. A formal declaration of war was never made by any participating nation; the Korean War was referred to as a

MASH Units

Mobile army surgical hospitals, or MASH units, were first created in 1944 but not used extensively until the Korean War. Based on the idea that the sooner treatment begins, the more lives that can be saved, the sixty-bed MASH unit was designed to provide immediate surgical care for severely wounded soldiers. After being evacuated from the battlefield, wounded soldiers would arrive by ambulance or helicopter at the MASH unit, where they were treated with rapid, lifesaving surgery, blood transfusions, and antibiotics before being airlifted to a permanent care facility in a city or town. MASH units were called "mobile" units because most of the facilities, including the operating room, were actually tents that could be rapidly taken down and packed for quick evacuation in case the enemy came too close.

Typically, the MASH unit was staffed by ten to sixteen physicians, ten to twelve nurses, and ninety to one hundred enlisted corpsmen providing a variety of support services. Wounded soldiers would first be taken to a receiving facility for triage, where nurses would assess the severity of the wounds and decide which needed immediate attention and which could wait. The wounded then went to a preoperative tent, where they were prepared for surgery, then into the operating tent for surgery. Following a brief stay in the postoperative recovery area, they were then transported to a rear hospital for more thorough care.

During the Vietnam War, MASH units were largely replaced by an inflatable rubber facility called the Medical Unit, Self-contained Transportable hospital, or MUST unit.

"police action," but it was war nonetheless, and nurses responded.

Nurses in Korea

Soon after U.S. troops were sent to South Korea, 540 nurses from the Army Nurse Corps arrived. They worked and traveled with fighting units, in field hospitals, and in military hospitals. They also cared for the wounded in mobile army surgical hospitals, or MASH units, located only 8 to 20 miles (13 to 32km) from the fighting. They provided care for wounded soldiers as well as Korean civilians, including pregnant women, ill children, and orphans. The Navy Nurse Corps staffed three hospital ships off the Korean coast. The new Air Force Nurse

During the Korean War nurses not only provided care for wounded military personnel but also for Korean civilians such as pregnant women, ill children, and orphans.

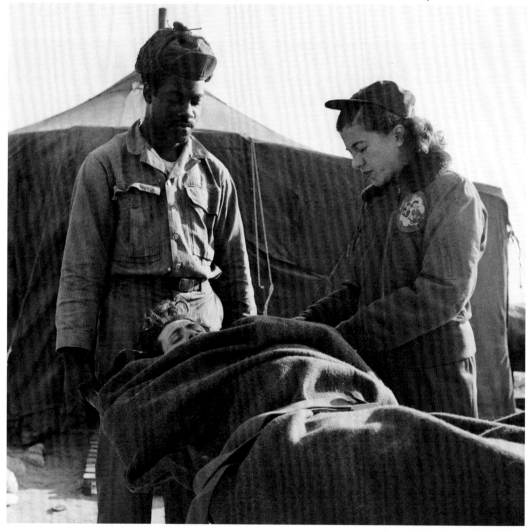

Corps, only one year old, sent two hundred flight nurses to assist with the care of wounded soldiers being evacuated to bases in South Korea and Japan. Their job was enormous; on one day, December 5, 1950, almost 4,000 soldiers were evacuated. By the end of the war, more than 350,000 patients had been evacuated by air.

Duty in Korea, as in all wars, was exhausting and difficult for the nurse. As described in an article commemorating the sixtieth anniversary of the war:

> These women far exceeded the normal scope of nursing practice as they independently triaged, started blood transfusions, initiated courses of penicillin and sutured wounds. They discharged logistical responsibilities by monitoring the supply chests and ordering replacement blood, oxygen and water. They improvised whenever supplies and equipment were not available, scrounging useful items from deserted family quarters or remaking discarded bits and pieces into functional tools. They managed overwhelming numbers of patients, regularly caring for 200 or more critically wounded soldiers and Marines in a 60-bed MASH. During rare quiet moments, they searched for strategies to improve their performance and avoid future blunders. In their limited off-duty hours, they assisted the long-suffering local populace. Usually, they carried out their mission in

stark settings with few resources. Adverse weather conditions were the norm. Extended periods of rain and mud were exceeded only by bitterly cold winters or sizzling hot summers. Field uniforms were scarce and woefully inadequate. The ill-fitting garments provided little protection in the frigid months and were unbearably hot during the sweltering summers.[29]

After thirty-seven months of fighting, very little progress had been made by either side. After almost twenty-eight thousand American deaths and 1.5 million enemy deaths, an armistice ending the fighting was signed in July 1953.

The Vietnam War (1965–1975)

Power struggles in the Southeast Asian country of Vietnam had been going on for decades between Vietnam, France, and Japan. In 1954, after both France and Japan left Vietnam, the country was divided into North and South Vietnam. As in Korea, conflicts continued between northern communist and southern anti-communist sides, each struggling for control. In the late 1950s the United States was firmly committed to preventing the spread of communism in Southeast Asia, and by 1962 there were thirty-two hundred military personnel in Vietnam as advisers to the South Vietnamese government.

In August 1964 North Vietnam attacked an American destroyer, the USS *Maddox*, in neutral waters. U.S. president

Lyndon Johnson responded by sending combat troops to Vietnam in February 1965. Although once again no formal declaration of war was ever made, the United States was essentially at war.

Nurses in Vietnam

American army nurses had been in Vietnam since 1956, when three nurses were sent on a temporary assignment to train South Vietnamese nurses in modern nursing practices. As the conflict worsened, many Americans became bitterly opposed to increased U.S. involvement in Southeast Asia, and there was very little support for the war at home. As a result, recruitment of nurses to serve in Vietnam was difficult. The first group of army nurses to arrive in Vietnam during wartime numbered only thirteen. Navy nurses served on two hospital ships offshore. As the fighting escalated over the next several years, more nurses were sent. In 1966 Congress passed a bill allowing men to join the Army, Navy, and Air Force Nurse Corps, and many male nurses were recruited.

By March 1973, when the last army nurses left Vietnam, more than six thousand nurses had served there. As in previous wars, the task of nursing in Vietnam was exhausting, dangerous, and emotionally draining. Nurses often worked around the clock to provide emergency care to large numbers of casualties. Wounds inflicted by modern weaponry were devastating. A new weapon called napalm, a highly flammable, gasoline-based gel launched from handheld launchers and planes, created enormous fires and caused massive burn injuries, often down to the bone. Besides treating battle wounds, nurses in the jungle environment of Vietnam dealt with illnesses such as malaria, cholera, leprosy, and bubonic plague, and they suffered bites from venomous snakes, spiders, and other native animals. Off-duty nurses often volunteered their services caring for civilians at orphanages and refugee centers and teaching Vietnamese physicians and nurses. There were no traditional "front lines," and nurses often found themselves in the midst of the fighting. Despite these dangers, only eight military nurses died during the Vietnam War, seven of them from accidents or illness and one from enemy fire.

War in the Twenty-First Century

Today nurses continue to serve in ongoing conflicts. Since 2001 the United States' involvement in wars in the central Asian nations of Iraq and Afghanistan have required the services of nurses from all branches of the military. In addition to caring for wounded soldiers on both sides, nurses in both countries have also cared for civilians and trained local nurses in more modern medical and nursing care. Nurses in these wars have faced hardships and challenges similar to those of previous wars. Writes Donahue, "Nurses serving in Iraq . . . endured unbearable heat, frequent mortar attacks, medical supply shortages, and sub-

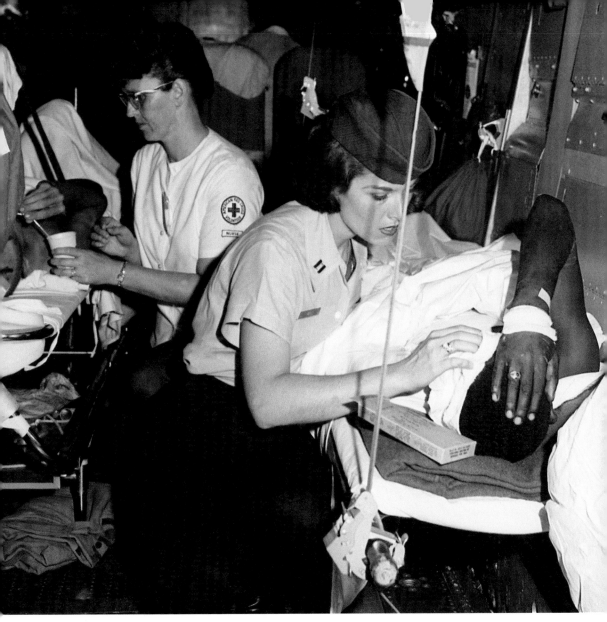

More than six thousand nurses served in the Vietnam War.

standard facilities. They have been stunned by the numbers and types of trauma cases they have seen. . . . They have witnessed courage in the face of injury and pain and loyalty in the face of grief, and they have provided comfort with the only thing left in many circumstances—human touch."[30]

Nurses who volunteer for service at war are courageous, dedicated professionals. The experience changes them in ways they could not have known before they went to war. "Nursing at war is a life changing experience that I would never trade," says navy nurse Tracie Brown, "but it wasn't the easiest either.

It was something special . . . something that changed me as a person and as a nurse."[31] First Lieutenant Mary C. Quinn, a Korean War veteran, says:

I learned different things about myself, where some of my weaknesses were, where some of my strengths were. I learned, I think, an awful lot more tolerance of other person's points of view. . . . I learned a lot from other people. I think that is one of the things about us being in the service, is that you are exposed to so many different people from so many different places. If you're wise, you can pick up a lot of good information from them. If you're not wise, then you become very regimented in your own thinking and you just never progress very far— tunnel vision. . . . I grew from that experience, both as a nurse and as a person.[32]

Chapter Five

Nursing in the Twentieth Century

The nineteenth century was a time of profound change and advancement in medicine, health care, and social awareness. During this time, nursing evolved from a menial, disrespected task performed by uneducated people into a highly respected profession with strict standards for education and practice. Most hospital nursing tasks, however, were still performed by students and included chores such as laundry, washing floors and walls, cooking meals, washing dishes, boiling water, filling kerosene lamps, carrying coal for the fireplace, sharpening needles, cleaning equipment, and rolling bandages. All this was in addition to patient care tasks such as bathing, administering medicines, feeding, dressing wounds, applying poultices, and assisting doctors in surgery.

During the twentieth century, significant advances in science and technology challenged nursing skill and education to keep pace and created many new roles, responsibilities, and opportunities for specialization for nurses. Nurses began to take responsibility for more complex tasks traditionally performed by physicians. These advances also presented nurses with new ethical and moral challenges never before encountered. In the latter part of the century, economic concerns became of great importance, as health care faced the need to control rapidly increasing costs while still providing quality care. The twentieth century served as a bridge between old ways of the past and new visions for the future of nursing.

Twentieth-Century Advances in Medicine

By World War II new antibiotics such as penicillin, streptomycin, and sulfa were being widely used. These drugs made surgery safer, made wound care more effective, and treated infectious diseases

Margaret Sanger

In the early years of the twentieth century, because of an 1873 law called the Comstock Act, it was illegal for physicians to provide birth control methods for women. Women who became pregnant sometimes sought illegal "back alley" abortions, performed by unlicensed people who provided no care afterward. Many women died from bleeding or infection after such procedures.

In 1913 a nurse named Margaret Sanger was working in New York's poor Lower East Side, often caring for women who had had many pregnancies or who sought back alley abortions. Sanger was outraged at the lack of legal birth control for these women. Her own mother had died at age fifty after eighteen pregnancies in twenty-two years.

In 1914 Sanger began publishing a newsletter called *The Woman Rebel* and a pamphlet called *Family Limitation*, in which she wrote about contraception and coined the term *birth control*. She was charged with violating the Comstock Act and fled to Europe to avoid going to jail. Back in the United States, however, support for her efforts grew. In 1916 the government dropped the charges against her, and she returned home. She opened a birth control clinic in Brooklyn, New York, the first in America. Almost immediately, she was arrested and spent thirty days in jail. In 1918, however, a higher court ruled that doctors could provide birth control to women if pregnancy would be dangerous for the woman. With the publicity of Sanger's trial and the new court ruling, support continued to grow.

Over the next several years, Sanger continued to work for contraceptive rights for women. In 1921 she formed the American Birth Control League, and in 1923 she

opened the first legal birth control clinic in the United States. In 1939 she served as president of the Birth Control Federation of America, which in 1942 became the Planned Parenthood Federation. Sanger served as its first president until she was eighty years old. In 1965 the Supreme Court struck down all remaining state laws against birth control. Sanger died the following year at age eighty-six.

In 1916 Margaret Sanger started a birth control clinic in New York City. She worked tirelessly her entire life for women's' reproductive rights and founded the organization that became the Planned Parenthood Federation.

such as tuberculosis. The development of insulin in the early 1920s offered a way to save the lives of thousands of patients with diabetes, a disorder of sugar metabolism. At about the same time, American physicians Jonas Salk and Albert Sabin were developing a vaccine for polio, a crippling disease that had disabled thousands of children. Nurses were responsible for administering these and other new drugs and for monitoring their effectiveness. Also by WWII, blood transfusions, developed during WWI, had become safer and more common. Nurses were responsible for administering blood to patients and watching them for signs of dangerous transfusion reactions.

The middle of the twentieth century saw the development of advanced methods for saving and prolonging life. Improvements in maternal and infant care meant that many more infants could now survive premature birth and birth defects that earlier would have been fatal. The discovery of the genetic molecule DNA led to an explosion in the understanding of many inherited illnesses and conditions such as sickle-cell anemia, cystic fibrosis, Down syndrome, and many others. Genetic science also created ways to develop thousands of new medicines, such as new antibiotics and antiviral drugs, and improved the safety of organ and tissue transplants. The treatment of cancer was revolutionized with radiation therapy, chemotherapy, and genetic therapies, and today cancer patients are living much longer and are often being cured of cancers that

were once fatal. Hemodialysis, a method of removing impurities from the blood, has saved the lives of untold numbers of people whose kidneys have failed.

New diagnostic technologies, such as ultrasound and CT and MRI scanning, catch health threats much earlier so that treatment is more effective. Advances in surgery, such as the heart-lung machine, laser surgery, robotics, and minimally invasive, or keyhole, surgery, permit surgeries that previously would never have been attempted. Technologically advanced methods for monitoring provide nurses with minute-by-minute data about their patient's heart rate, blood pressure, temperature, weight, fluid balance, blood oxygen level, intracranial (inside the skull) pressure, level of consciousness, and many other indicators of the patient's condition. All of these advances altered what nurses do and how they do it.

As medicine and surgery became more complex, nurses were required to learn a great deal of new information, become more expert at monitoring their patient's conditions, and manage increasingly complex technologies. Nurses, like physicians, found it necessary to specialize in one or two areas in order to maintain a high level of expertise in the increasingly complex field of health care. Intensive care units, for patients needing close supervision around the clock, began to appear in hospitals as separate units, and the specialty role of critical care nurse evolved. Other specialty areas such as long-term care, surgery, postoperative recovery rooms, burn units, dialysis units, and orthopedic, neurology, psychiatric, and oncology (cancer) units appeared, creating more nursing specialties.

Advanced Practice Nursing

In 1965 the federal government allowed funding for two new health insurance plans that would help pay for health care for the poor (Medicaid) and the elderly (Medicare). With hundreds of thousands more Americans able to access health care, the workload for physicians expanded rapidly, and they began to delegate some of their tasks to nurses. At the same time, nurses were becoming more aware of their high level of skill and expertise. In some areas their scope of skill and knowledge was actually greater than that of younger doctors. Nurses in many settings, especially nurse anesthetists and nurse-midwives, began to practice more independently of the physician, making their own clinical judgments and decisions about care. These nurses became known as advanced practice nurses.

Two models of advanced practice nursing appeared. The nursing model, or clinical nurse specialist (CNS), had first appeared in the late 1950s and focused on education and nursing functions in a specific specialty, such as psychiatry. The collaborative model refers to advanced practice nurses who have postgraduate-level training in medical and biological sciences as well as nursing. They often work with physicians to plan and direct care. Nurse anesthetists and nurse-midwives are examples of collaborative nursing roles.

A newer collaborative role, first appearing in the 1960s, is that of the nurse practitioner. Nurse practitioners (NPs) are nurses who carry out many of the functions traditionally done by physicians. They may work in a physician's office, or they may run their own clinics, especially in outlying areas. They are seen as equal partners with the physician. They perform complex health assessments, prescribe treatment, evaluate the effectiveness of treatment, and design thorough plans of care. As nurses, they are trained to treat not only the physical needs of patients but their emotional, social, and educational needs as well. The tasks they are allowed to perform vary greatly, depending on state laws. For example, eighteen states allow NPs to work completely independently of physicians; eight states allow them to prescribe medications but not to diagnose or treat illness without physician involvement. The other twenty-four states require physician involvement in all three areas. NPs do not perform surgery, but they may perform procedures such as lumbar punctures, Pap smears, or bone marrow biopsies.

In some areas of the country, the NP movement was resisted by physicians who felt that nurses should remain subservient to the physician, but the movement progressed rapidly in the 1970s as the federal government and private donors provided more funding for NP education programs. It continued to gain momentum in the 1980s and 1990s, as the issues of health-care costs and a shortage of primary care physicians

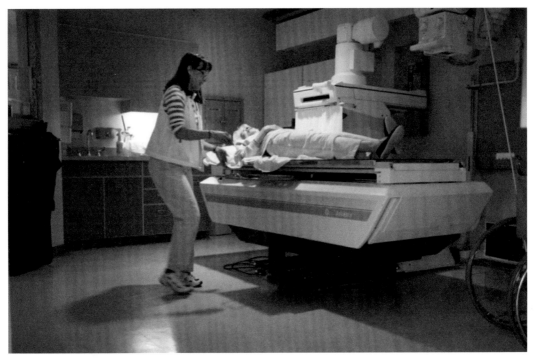

A technician takes X-rays of an elderly patient. The complexity of modern health care has been met by many nurses' being trained in other medical fields, which is known as advanced practice nursing.

(family doctors) became critical. As NP programs increased in number, CNS programs began to decline. Today NPs specialize in pediatrics, adult care, family health, critical care, geriatrics (care of the elderly), and rural health care.

Nursing Education in the Twentieth Century

With new roles for nurses opening up in the twentieth century, the challenge arose for nursing education to provide adequate training for these new roles. In addition, significant changes in American society around the turn of the twentieth century, such as the economic shift from agriculture to industry and the influx of millions of European immi-

grants, made it necessary to upgrade the quality of the nursing profession.

At the beginning of the century, inadequate schools of nursing still existed in the United States. The first state licensure laws, passed in 1903, set high standards for nursing practice and education. Licensure set educated nurses apart from uneducated ones, which helped protect the safety of patients. Another important change in education was the introduction of preparatory classroom courses that students would have to take before beginning actual work with patients. The first such program was begun in 1901 at Johns Hopkins Hospital in Baltimore. After the courses were completed, the students would then

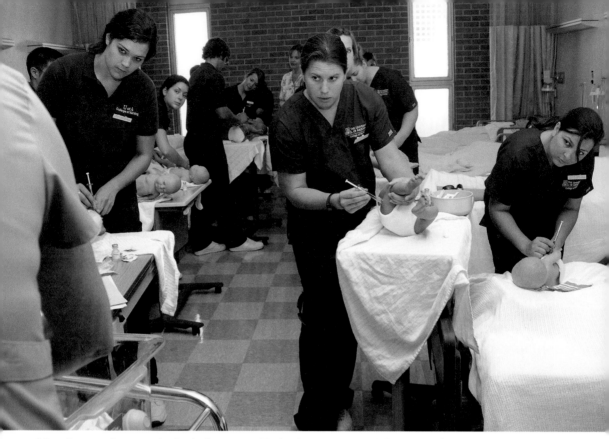

Nursing students train for infant care. Today's nurses specialize in pediatrics, adult and critical care, geriatrics, family health, and other areas of health care.

enter the hospital, but as students rather than as employees.

Nursing education also began to provide opportunities for higher levels of achievement. In 1919 the first four-year bachelor of science in nursing degree program was offered at the University of Minnesota. In 1922 six nursing students at Indiana University created the first national honor society for nursing students, Sigma Theta Tau. The organization supports excellence in nursing scholarship, nursing research, and leadership. In 1956 the Columbia University School of Nursing became the first to offer a master's degree in nursing. At first, the master's degree prepared

nurses to be educators or administrators. After the CNS and NP roles were developed, however, it allowed nurses to get an advanced nursing education in a clinical role involving direct patient care.

Nursing Research and Literature

As twentieth-century nurses began to recognize the importance of education, they also began to recognize the importance of creating their own body of nursing knowledge through research. Research is the search for new learning through careful, systematic observation and experimentation. It is used to add new knowledge, confirm the results of earlier research, solve problems, or come up with better ways of doing things. Florence Nightingale was ahead of her time in the field of nursing research, because she based her reforms during and after the Crimean War on careful observation, fact gathering, and statistical reports.

When Nightingale's education model was adopted in the United States, however, her use of research did not come

Three nurses hold their diplomas after graduating from a nursing school in 1915. New roles and an expanded need for nurses made it necessary to upgrade the quality of nursing education.

with it. The environment of American schools was generally one of strict obedience to physicians and other superiors; critical thinking and questioning were not encouraged. One early exception was Alice Magaw (1860–1928), an American nurse anesthetist who published five research articles about anesthetics between 1899 and 1906, all of which appeared in medical journals.

Although early twentieth-century nursing leaders saw the need for a body of nursing research, efforts at the time were focused on improving nursing education. Research was being done, but most of the work was done by phy-

The Hospice Movement

In the twentieth century, as more and more attention was being paid to keeping people alive, nurses began to realize that the needs of those who were dying were being neglected. In response to this need, the hospice movement began to take shape. According to the Hospice Foundation of America:

> Hospice is a special concept of care designed to provide comfort and support to patients and their families when a life-limiting illness no longer responds to cure-oriented treatments. Hospice care neither prolongs life nor hastens death. Hospice staff and volunteers offer a specialized knowledge of medical care, including pain management. The goal of hospice care is to improve the quality of a patient's last days by offering comfort and dignity.

Hospice provides emotional, social, and spiritual support for the patient and the family and provides grief counseling before and after the patient's death.

One of the first nurses to focus her practice on the needs of the dying patient was British nurse Cicely Saunders (1918–2005). Saunders worked at several private homes for the dying, mostly charitable religious homes, but eventually decided to open one where people of any faith would feel welcome. In 1967 Saunders, now a physician, opened Saint Christopher's Hospice in London. In the United States the first hospice was established by Florence Wald (1917–2008; no relation to Lillian Wald of the Henry Street Settlement), after hearing a talk given by Saunders. She traveled to London in 1969 to work at Saint Christopher's and to study the effects of hospice care. She opened her hospice in New Haven, Connecticut, in 1974. Today there are more than forty-seven hundred hospice programs in the United States.

Hospice Foundation of America. "What Is Hospice?," 2012. www.hospicefoundation.org/whatishospice.

sicians and others who were not nurses. An exception was American nurse Isabel M. Stewart (1878–1963), who felt that nursing students ought to be taught the research process. Stewart, who wrote extensively on the need for nursing research to be done by nurses, said:

> If nursing is ever to justify its name as an applied science, if it is ever to free itself from these old, superficial, haphazard methods, some way must be found to submit all our practices as rapidly as possible to the most searching tests which modern science can devise. . . . There is not much use waiting for someone outside our own body to recognize our critical situation and to offer to do the work for us. Some help may be secured from physicians and from experts in other fields, but most of the experimentation that is done will have to be carried on in all probability by our own members.[33]

Beginning in the 1930s, nursing research began to become a larger part of the profession. After World War II, government funding for nursing research projects was made available through the U.S. Department of Health, Education, and Welfare. In 1950 the ANA conducted research to study nursing functions in different settings and nurses' relationships with coworkers. In 1955 the American Nurses Foundation was set up as part of the ANA to provide funding for nursing research studies and publication. Other private and government sources of funding for research followed over the next two decades. In the 1970s, nursing research was included in all college nursing education programs in the United States, and in 1986 the National Center for Nursing Research was established.

With the rise in nursing research came the expansion of published nursing literature and nursing journals, which provided a way to communicate new knowledge to nurses all over the United States and the world. The first nursing journal, called *Nightingale*, was published in 1886. In 1900 the first issue of *American Journal of Nursing* appeared, and it eventually became the official journal of the ANA. Other nursing journals followed, such as *Nursing Outlook* and *Nursing Research*. Today there are journals for almost every specialty and subspecialty of nursing, such as *Cancer Nursing Practice, Issues in Mental Health Nursing, AORN Journal* for surgical nurses, *Journal of Orthopedic Nursing*, and many others. Nurses also publish textbooks and reference books, and today there are several thousand general and specialized textbooks for nurses in print.

Philosophical and Ethical Issues in Nursing

Twentieth-century advances in medical knowledge and technologies allowed physicians and nurses to provide a multitude of new treatments and procedures to their patients. Sometimes, however, these new possibilities ran counter to certain societal values, standards, and

In 1955 the American Nurses Foundation was created to provide funding for nursing research and publications.

philosophies about what is right and wrong. Questions arose about whether or not certain measures were ethical—whether or not they ought to be done simply because they could be done.

The term *bioethics* was coined in 1927 to refer to health-related issues that can be controversial because of these ques-tions. Certain issues in particular pre-sented (and still present) ethical and moral dilemmas for health-care provid-ers in general and for nurses in particu-lar. One of the most significant bioethi-cal challenges for nurses in the twentieth century was, and continues to be, the issue of a patient's right to die.

Euthanasia and the Right to Die

Euthanasia is the practice of intentionally ending a life in order to end pain and suffering, either actively by hastening the death or passively by allowing the death to occur naturally. Euthanasia is commonly done for ill or injured animals. Euthanasia for humans has been practiced in various forms since ancient times, but only since the seventeenth century has it had a medical meaning, with a physician involved in ending the life of a suffering patient.

The modern debate over the ethics of euthanasia began in the 1870s. At that time, a schoolteacher named Samuel Williams said in a speech to a group of philosophical thinkers:

> In all cases of hopeless and painful illness it should be the recognized duty of the medical attendant, whenever so desired by the patient, to administer chloroform, or such other anesthetic . . . so as to destroy consciousness at once, and put the sufferer at once to a quick and painless death; all needful precautions being adopted to prevent any possible abuse of such duty and means being taken to establish, beyond the possibility of doubt or question, that the remedy was applied at the express wish of the patient.[34]

By the middle of the twentieth century, medical procedures and technologies such as cardiopulmonary resuscitation (CPR), surgically implanted feeding tubes, and mechanical ventilators were being widely used to save and prolong lives that earlier would have ended from illness or injury. For example, patients who had sustained severe head injuries could be kept alive but in a state of unconsciousness, or coma, with a ventilator providing mechanical breathing and feeding tubes providing nutrition and hydration. Depending on the severity of the injury, the coma could be permanent, but the patient would still be considered alive as long as the heart was still beating. Ethical questions arose about human dignity and what it means to die a "good death"—was it morally right to keep a person alive artificially when there was no hope of recovery? What would the patient have wanted? Who has the right to make this decision for the patient when the patient cannot make the decision him- or herself? What personal and religious factors have to be considered when making such a difficult decision? For nurses questions arose about whether or not the nurse must participate in these decisions if he or she strongly disagrees with them.

In 1975 a twenty-one-year-old New Jersey woman named Karen Ann Quinlan became unconscious and stopped breathing after taking the sedative drug Valium and drinking alcohol at a party. She was not found for about fifteen minutes. Paramedics performed CPR and took her to the hospital, but she did not wake up. She was put on a mechanical ventilator, but tests showed that she was in a "persistent vegetative state"—an irreversible coma. After several months her family made the difficult decision to remove her from the ventilator. Hospital officials refused to allow it, however, for fear of being charged with homicide. In a widely publicized case, the Quinlans went to the New Jersey Supreme Court, which ruled in their favor. The ventilator was removed, but surprisingly, Quinlan continued to breathe on her own. For nine more years she was kept alive with artificial nutrition, until she died from pneumonia in 1985.

The Quinlan case served to define a patient's right to die under his or her

The parents of Karen Ann Quinlan went to the New Jersey Supreme Court to secure the right to remove their daughter's ventilator in a controversial case that brought euthanasia into public debate.

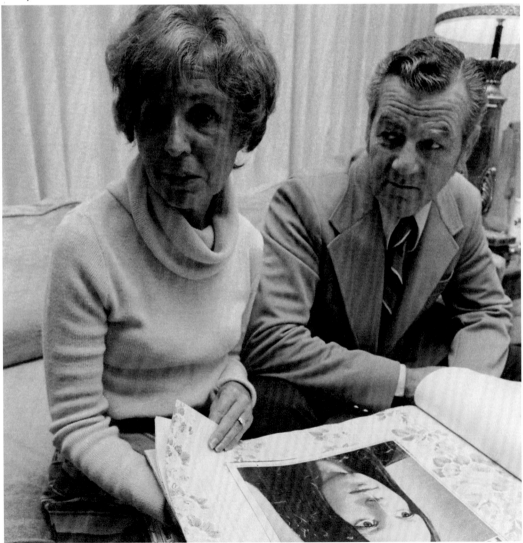

The AIDS Epidemic and Nursing Practice

Perhaps no development of the twentieth century has affected nursing practice more than the appearance of the human immunodeficiency virus (HIV), which causes the disease called acquired immunodeficiency syndrome, or AIDS. The virus first became prevalent in the early 1980s, affecting mostly young homosexual men. Nurse practitioner Carl Kirton writes:

> Almost overnight, health care workers were confronted with caring for individuals with a communicable disease that they knew very little about, and in a population with which they were generally unfamiliar. Many health care workers were conflicted by this new disease and the people who were affected by it. They struggled with their fears, their attitudes, their prejudices, and sometimes their own mortality.

Early in the epidemic, when little was known about HIV/AIDS, there was no treatment for the disease, and it was almost always fatal. Fear led many health-care workers to refuse to care for HIV-positive patients. As more was learned about its transmission by exposure to blood and body fluids, precautions were developed to help protect health-care workers from risk of exposure. Nurses and other health workers routinely wear personal protective equipment such as disposable gloves, masks, eyewear, and gowns. Needles and other sharp objects are manufactured with safety guards and are handled very carefully to avoid accidental sticks or cuts. Surgical procedures have improved in ways that keep blood loss and exposure to a minimum.

Today, despite tremendous advances in the understanding of the transmission and management of HIV/AIDS, the illness remains a significant global health issue. In 2011 more than 2.5 million new cases were reported worldwide. Today more than 40 million people live with HIV, and about 10 percent of them are children under fifteen. From the beginning of the epidemic, nurses have been deeply committed to caring for HIV/AIDS patients. For example, in 1987 the Association of Nurses in AIDS Care was founded to respond to the epidemic, with nurses around the world working in HIV/AIDS care, research, prevention, education, and governmental policy making.

Carl Kirton. "Nurses at the Forefront of a Pandemic: HIV/AIDS Nurses." *NSNA Imprint*, April/May 2012, p. 54.

own terms, and the right of the family to make that decision if the patient is unable to do so. As a result, health-care institutions began to form ethics committees to address issues such as this. The medical and legal professions developed a definition of death based on brain function. In order to avoid such controversy in their own lives, people began to make their own wishes known through legal documents such as living wills and advance care directives.

A similar case occurred in 1983, when a twenty-five-year-old Missouri woman named Nancy Cruzan lost control of her car and was thrown out into a water-filled ditch by the side of the road. By the time she was found, she had stopped breathing and her heart had stopped beating. Paramedics restored her heart-beat, but, like Quinlan, the lack of oxygen to her brain had left her in a persistent vegetative state. Also like Quinlan, Cruzan continued to breathe after she was disconnected from the ventilator. Unlike in the Quinlan case, however, Cruzan's parents eventually asked that her feeding tube also be removed, even though they realized it would lead to her death by starvation and dehydration. The hospital refused to allow this, and a long court battle began between her parents and the state of Missouri. After the Cruzans provided proof to the court that their daughter would not have wanted to be kept alive in that condition, the U.S. Supreme Court ruled in favor of the family. The feeding tube was removed in December 1990, and Cruzan died twelve days later.

Cases such as these, made possible by modern medical knowledge and technology, may present serious ethical challenges to nurses, who are charged with providing quality care for their patients. Nurses may be called upon to provide dying cancer patients with large amounts of narcotic pain medication to ease their suffering, even though they know it may hasten the patients' death. Nurses may be reluctant to provide life-prolonging treatment to a patient whose family wants everything possible to be done to keep the patient alive even though it may prolong the patient's suffering. Organizations such as the End-of-Life Nursing Consortium, the Euthanasia Research and Guidance Organization, and the National Hospice Organization exist to help patients and health professionals deal with end-of-life issues such as these.

Looking to the Future

At the beginning of the twentieth century, the major challenge for nursing was to establish itself as a credible profession, respected by patients, physicians, and government policy makers. Nursing leaders accomplished this goal by setting high standards for nursing education, competence, and quality of care. Today nursing is what it set out to be—a highly regarded career for both men and women around the world. As nursing progresses in the twenty-first century, new challenges for nursing await in terms of demand for nurses, nursing education, economic concerns, health-care reform, and many more areas.

Chapter Six

Challenges for the Future

At the beginning of the twenty-first century, nurses face challenges and opportunities that Florence Nightingale could never have envisioned. Advanced medical technologies and new drugs allow people to live much longer than ever before; the average life expectancy today is more than eighty-one years for women and seventy-nine years for men. Expensive technologies, a growing and aging population, and serious health issues such as obesity and smoking place immense demands on the health-care system. At the same time, a growing shortage of nurses, rapidly rising health-care costs, and reforms in the nation's health-care system present challenges for nursing to maintain high standards for education and high-quality care.

An Aging Patient Population

Shortly after the return of American troops from World War II, the United States experienced a sharp increase in population that came to be called the baby boom. Approximately 79 million American babies were born between 1946 and 1964. Today the first of the baby boomers are in their mid- to late sixties and beginning to retire. In addition, because of the remarkable advances in medical science and technology made in the twentieth century, baby boomers are living much longer than their parents did. Together these two factors mean that the American health-care system will soon be caring for a very large number of people over age sixty-five.

According to the National League for Nursing, "By 2020 more than twenty percent of the American population will be 65 and over, with those over 85 constituting the fastest growing age group."[35] An older population that is living for many more years than in previous decades presents challenges to the health-care system in several ways. First,

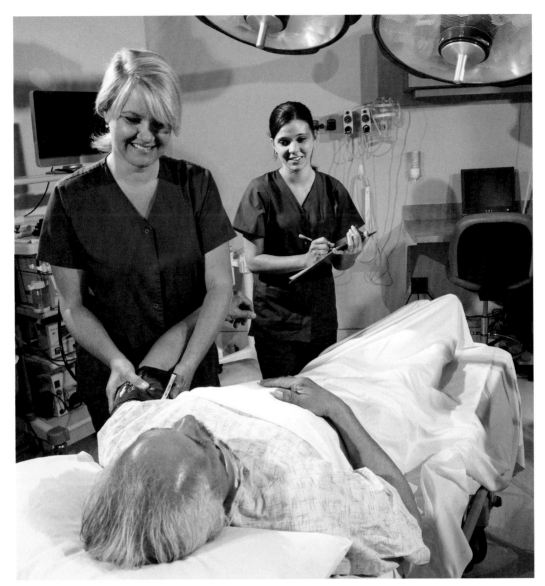

By 2020 more than one-fifth of the U.S. population will be sixty-five or older, which will challenge nursing and health-care facilities because people experience more health problems as they age.

as people age, they experience more chronic, or long-term, health problems than do younger people, including such illnesses as high blood pressure, heart and blood vessel disease, diabetes, Alzheimer's disease, and others. Costly new drugs and expensive medical technology are available to help manage these health issues, but the demand for these resources means that health-care costs are skyrocketing, and government spending on Medicare, the federal insurance program for people over sixty-five, is increasing rapidly. The rising cost of health care due to an aging population and new medical technology creates a challenge for nurses to continue to provide high-quality care while keeping costs under control.

Another way in which the baby boom has challenged health care is in terms of the number of registered nurses (RNs) available to care for an expanding and aging patient population. "The combination of the aging of the Baby Boom generation and the increase in life expectancy is going to yield a doubling of the numbers of older people," says John W. Rowe, professor of health policy and management at Columbia University in New York. "And it's important to understand that older people themselves account for a disproportionate amount of the utilization of health care resources."[36]

A Shortage of Nurses

There are almost 3 million nurses in the United States. Nurses form the largest single segment of the health-care workforce, but there is currently a growing shortage of RNs available to care for America's aging population. According to a 2009 study, the shortage of nurses in the United States is predicted to grow to as many as 260,000 by 2025. Two major factors have contributed to the shortage of nurses—one related to new nurses coming into the profession, the other related to older nurses leaving it.

First, enrollment in nursing schools is not keeping up with the demand for well-trained nurses. In the past, new enrollees were young women right out of high school. Today, however, there are many other career options available for young women, who traditionally make up the majority of those attending nursing school, and fewer of them are choosing nursing as a career. The average age of the new nursing student is rising, as many young women delay entering a career in nursing while they raise children or work in other jobs.

To make matters worse, many of those who do apply to nursing schools are being turned away, largely for economic reasons. Before the 1970s most nurses were trained in hospital-based programs. They got most of their training from experienced nurses and by working as employees in the hospital. Since that time, however, more and more nurses are being trained in university or college programs, creating a need for more nurse educators, more classroom space, and up-to-date technology. Budget constraints, however, limit the numbers of faculty and resources available to nursing programs. As a result of decreased enrollment and increased costs, there are not enough students currently in the nursing education system to replace the ones who are leaving the workforce.

Many experienced nurses who have been in practice for years are leaving the profession, for several reasons. Over the last two decades, wages for nurses have not kept pace with the rising cost of living, and many nurses have left nursing for better-paying opportunities in other fields. In 2002 there were nearly five hundred thousand nurses employed in careers other than nursing, and a 2007 study showed that 13 percent of new nurses changed their career after only one year.

Job dissatisfaction creates another reason nurses are leaving. Nursing is much more complicated and stressful than it was even twenty years ago. The shortage of working nurses makes the workday more stressful and exhausting for those still on the job, and many have to work extra shifts and put in overtime. Most nurses feel that this has a negative impact on the quality of care patients receive. Many studies have shown a significant connection between nurse staffing levels and quality of care, patient safety, and even mortality rates.

A third reason for the loss of experienced nurses is that, as younger women choose other careers, the average age of nurses is rising. Those in their fifties are the fastest-growing age group of nurses, and as older nurses who are baby boomers themselves begin to retire, they are being replaced with younger, less-experienced nurses. This means that not only is there a growing shortage of nurses in general, there is also a growing shortage of experienced nurses in particular.

A major challenge for nursing, then, is how to address the shortage of nurses in the face of the rising demand for health care. The responsibility for dealing with this challenge falls largely on nursing education and on state and federal governments.

Addressing the Nursing Shortage

Nursing schools across the country are employing a variety of strategies to attract and retain new students. Some are forming partnerships with hospitals to offer hospital employees ways to get a nursing education that costs less and fits better into busy work and family schedules. For example, one school in Minnesota has partnered with a nearby hospital to offer its employees the opportunity to advance their education through online courses at a reduced cost. This kind of program requires fewer faculty members, and employees of the hospital can work toward a bachelor's, master's, and even a doctorate and still be able to work full-time. Other hospitals help by paying a portion of the salaries for nursing educators, helping their employees pay nursing school tuition, and providing flexible schedules so that employees can work and still attend classes.

Governments are also working to ease the nursing shortage. For example, many state governments are partnering with private corporations to provide money for faculty salaries, new and updated educational facilities, and tuition support for students. The federal government also supports nursing education through the Title VIII Nursing Workforce Development program, which provides funding to support education for advanced practice nurses, NPs, public health nurses, and nursing educators. It also provides funding to help economically disadvantaged and

The Future of Men in Nursing

One of the recommendations made in the Robert Wood Johnson report on the future of nursing was for nurse leaders to create a more diverse nursing workforce in order to meet the needs of an increasingly diverse patient population. In addition to attracting more students of varied racial and ethnic backgrounds, there is also a push to increase the number of men in nursing.

In the nineteenth century, largely as a result of wars, women took on the role of caring for the male soldiers, and nursing became a female-dominated occupation. Beginning in the 1970s, as women began to explore other career opportunities, more men began to enter nursing, but they were often not allowed to work in women's health fields such as obstetrics and gynecology. They dealt with discrimination from female instructors and students and with lack of support from those who saw them as "effeminate" or "not good enough to be a doctor."

In 1980 the American Assembly of Men in Nursing was created "to encourage men of all ages to become nurses, to support men who are in the nursing profession, to advocate for further research regarding men in nursing, and to support members' full participation in the nursing profession," according to the organization. Although some gender bias persists today, cultural attitudes are changing rapidly, and the number of men entering nursing is increasing. According to the American Association of Colleges of Nursing, in the 2010–2011 school year, more than 11 percent of students in four-year nursing programs were men. Men are attracted to nursing because of the flexible hours, good pay, and opportunities for research and career advancement. The nursing shortage has helped open up the field to men, but at only 8 percent, they are still underrepresented in the nursing profession. As nursing continues to evolve, men will continue to play an important role in its development.

Nursing programs have seen a rise in the number of male students.

Quoted in Men in Nursing. "Men in Nursing: Past, Present, and Future," 2006. http://men innursingpastpresentandfuture.blogspot .com/2007/02/men-in-nursing-past-present -and-future.html#history.

Nursing graduates pose for a graduation photo. The nursing shortage has been addressed by the federal government through supporting nursing education funding and development programs.

minority students and provides scholarships and loans to students in return for a two-year commitment to work in hospitals that are experiencing a critical shortage of nurses. It also provides financial support for nurses who work in geriatrics, or the care of the elderly.

Other Trends in Nursing Education

Nursing education faces other challenges for change in addition to addressing the nursing shortage. The rapid growth in information technology over the last twenty years has dramatically changed the way health information is gathered, stored, accessed, and shared. Most health-care institutions have switched from handwritten patient care records to digital records, which can be accessed from computers throughout the institution or from the doctor's office or home computer. X-rays and other diagnostic information can also be stored and accessed electronically and sent to specialists anywhere in the world. Portable handheld devices perform diagnostic tests that previously could only be done in a laboratory. Information technology, especially use of the Internet, has also greatly changed the way patients get health information. Telemedicine technology allows patients and physicians instant access to one another without either one having to travel. Nurses in the future must be able to use all kinds of information technology with competence, and nursing schools will be called upon to provide education in this area.

In past decades, care revolved around the physician as the "captain of the ship," assessing the patient and writing orders, and the nurse carrying out those orders. As health care becomes

Telemedicine

As part of the effort to improve care and reduce costs, the use of telemedicine, also called telehealth or e-health, is expanding. Telemedicine technology allows doctors and nurses to evaluate, diagnose, and advise patients without going to the patient's home. They can monitor information such as heart rate and rhythm, blood pressure, temperature, blood sugar and other blood data, medication use, pacemaker function, and more. The technology allows patients to communicate with doctors and nurses without having to travel to the office or the hospital. It also allows health professionals to communicate with each other and get immediate answers, information, and advice from experts anywhere in the world.

Telemedicine technologies can be used to transmit data, sound, and images such as X-rays and CT scans by using telecommunications technology such as telephone lines, computers, television cables, or satellite links. It can be sent live so that the receiving person can participate at the time the information is being collected, or it can be stored and sent at a later time.

Telemedicine has many kinds of uses. It is useful in rural areas where patients live far from health-care facilities and where hospitals are smaller and may not have the experts they need on staff. It can be used in schools, prisons, workplaces, and for emergencies on ships or planes. It is useful in developing countries or very remote places where there may be a shortage or absence of health care. It can also be used in disaster areas where the need for care is great and health facilities may be unavailable. Home care nurses can use telemedicine technology to "visit" their patients using video conferencing, online chats, or video phones.

A U.S. radiologist uses telemedicine equipment to aid a doctor in the Philippines.

more and more complex, quality care of the patient now requires the involvement of many kinds of care providers, with expertise in many specialized areas. Care of a patient is now more of a collaborative effort, with teams of providers such as specialty physicians, advanced practice nurses, dieticians, pharmacists, social workers, home health nurses, wound care specialists, and others all working together toward a good outcome for the patient. Nurses in the future will need to be familiar with all these roles and know how to work effectively as part of a larger team. Nursing education programs will need to provide opportunities for students to develop this kind of knowledge and skill.

The further development of nursing research is another area of challenge for nursing education. Nursing research provides a sound, scientific basis for the decisions that nurses make about patient care. Nursing research studies provide information about the health habits of the public, the effectiveness of treatment methods, how to help patients and families manage health problems effectively, how to include emotional and spiritual considerations into health care, ways to promote illness prevention and health maintenance, ways to make health-care delivery more efficient and cost-effective, and much more. Nursing schools, especially university-based programs, can provide opportunities for undergraduate and graduate students to experience the research process.

Health-Care Reform in the Twenty-First Century

As health-care costs continue to skyrocket, good health care and health insurance become more difficult for people to afford. Many millions of Americans have limited or no access to quality health care because they make too much money to qualify for Medicaid but do not make enough to be able to afford private health insurance. Government policy makers as well as regular citizens recognize that the American health-care system is in need of improvement to address the issues of cost and accessibility of health care. Nurses are deeply involved in helping make decisions about the best ways to make the needed changes. Nurses and nursing practice are, and in the future will continue to be, greatly affected by these changes.

In March 2010, after much controversy and debate, Congress passed and President Barack Obama signed into law the Patient Protection and Affordable Care Act (PPACA). This sweeping legislation provides for many major changes in how health care is delivered and paid for in America. While not universal health care, the law is designed to make it possible for as many as 30 million uninsured Americans to have health insurance. It also aims to control the rising costs of health care. It is controversial, however, because it affects every aspect of health care, including hospitals, insurance companies, health-care providers, and patients, and because it will cost a great deal of money to put all of its provisions into effect.

On March 23, 2010, President Barack Obama signed the Patient Protection and Affordable Health Care Act into law. The legislation provides for major changes in how health care is delivered and paid for in America.

The PPACA has important meaning for the nursing profession. The sharp increase in the number of insured people means that many more people will be seeking health care. In the face of a rapidly aging population of baby boomers and an already growing shortage of nurses, the need to serve all patients with quality care while keeping costs under control will be an enormous challenge. There is also predicted to be a severe shortage of primary care physicians such as family doctors, who see the patient first. This means that advanced practice nurses such as NPs and nurse-midwives will be called upon to help fill the need for primary care providers.

The Future of Nursing Report

Because the nursing profession is so profoundly affected by changes in health-care policy, nursing leaders saw a need to have as much input into the decision making as possible. In 2008, two years before the PPACA was passed, the Institute of Medicine and the Robert Wood Johnson Foundation (RWJF), which provides financial support for health-care issues, began a two-year project to examine the nursing profession and make recommendations that would address how the profession needs to change in order to meet the challenges of the future. In 2010 the RWJF released a report called *The Future of Nursing: Leading Change, Advancing Health*. The six-hundred-page report offers several important recommendations for how nurses, hospitals, government agencies, and others can help meet future demands in a changing health-care environment.

The report focuses on four key messages. The first is about improving and increasing nursing education. The report discusses ways to help new nurses make the transition from school to practice so that fewer nurses leave the profession. It also recommends increasing the percentage of nurses having at least a bachelor of science degree (four-year college degree) from 50 percent to 80 percent by 2020. It also recommends doubling the number of nurses with a doctoral degree, currently less than 1 percent of all nurses, by 2020 in order to add nurses in advanced practice, teaching, and research.

The second key message involves allowing nurses at all levels to practice to the fullest extent of their training. For example, state laws and hospital regulations regarding what tasks advanced practice nurses can and cannot perform vary widely from state to state. The report stresses the importance of streamlining regulations so that nurses

can be allowed to perform all the skills they are trained to do. This is somewhat controversial—many physicians are concerned about nurses moving into practice areas traditionally held by physicians. Nursing leaders, however, stress that this change would help fill the need for primary care providers as well as reduce health-care costs. "We don't have the primary care providers to care for those people, so I think the demand for nurse practitioners will grow astronomically,"[37] said Karen Haller, vice president of nursing at Johns Hopkins Hospital.

The third key message is about creating a health-care culture in which nurses collaborate as full and equal partners with physicians and other health-care professionals in a team approach to care. One way this might be accomplished is for universities to streamline the academic calendars of their schools of nursing, medicine, and other health professions so that students can participate in classes with each other. Being a full partner also includes the need for nurses to take a more active role in policy making and problem solving. "To be effective in [their new] roles, nurses must see policy as something they can shape rather than something that happens to them,"[38] says the report. "The health care reform debate has really energized nurses," adds Cheryl Peterson, director of the ANA's department of nursing practice and policy. "They are contacting their members of Congress, have been engaged in that debate and attended the town hall meetings at the local level."[39]

Health-Care Reform in America

Reform in America's health-care system has been a topic of political debate since the early part of the twentieth century. During the Great Depression of the 1930s, when many Americans could not afford health care, President Franklin Roosevelt attempted to provide for government-sponsored health-care programs for all Americans (universal health care) as part of his new Social Security law. Opposition from the American Medical Association, however, led him to remove the programs from the bill. At this time, hospital, physician groups, and employers began to offer health insurance programs. After World War II, President Harry Truman also attempted to establish universal health care, but this attempt also failed. In 1965 the Medicare and Medicaid programs were enacted, which provide government health insurance to those over age sixty-five and to those in economic hardship. By the late 1970s health-care costs had started to rise at a very rapid rate. Presidents Nixon, Carter, and Clinton all tried to pass versions of universal health care, but none were successful.

By the end of the twentieth century, health-care costs had risen so fast that many employers could no longer afford to provide insurance for their employees. An estimated 45 million Americans who were too young for Medicare and whose incomes were too high to qualify for Medicaid were left without health insurance because they could not afford to buy insurance on their own. Health-care and health insurance availability were major issues in both the 2008 and 2012 presidential elections.

The fourth focus is on collecting information about the nursing workforce. The report identifies a need for more reliable data on how many and what kinds of health-care professionals are currently employed, where they are employed, and what types of activities they perform. This kind of information would help identify areas of greatest need, assess the impact of health-care reforms on the nursing workforce, and reduce wasted time and money by identifying where different kinds of professionals might be doing the same kinds of activities.

Following the release of the report, the RWJF teamed up with the American Association of Retired Persons to form the Future of Nursing: Campaign for Action to start work on making these recommendations happen. According to the campaign's website, it focuses on nursing and "envisions a nation where all Americans have access to high-quality, patient-centered care in a health care system where nurses contribute as essential partners in achieving success."[40]

Nursing leaders see the RWJF report as a good start toward growth in the nursing profession. "I think it's a good blueprint for the future," says Catherine L. Gillis, president of the American Academy of Nursing. "I don't think any group has a lock on advocacy, and I don't believe that any one group is restricted from reaching out and being in the patient's world, making home visits, doing a little something out of the ordinary."[41]

Other Trends in Nursing

In addition to addressing the nursing shortage, new directions for nursing education, the rise in medical technologies, and the changes recommended in the RWJF report, the profession in the twenty-first century may see other trends that are closely tied to what is happening in health care. First, as efforts are made to control health-care costs, there will be a push to keep patients out of the hospital. Nurses can help with this by continuing to follow patients after they have left the hospital to make sure they are taking proper care of themselves. They can do this through home visits, phone calls, or by using telemedicine technology. "Keeping patients healthy so that they aren't in the hospital is the right thing to do," says Joyce Ramsey-Coleman, chief nursing officer with Children's Healthcare of Atlanta. "If my blood pressure goes up and I'm not checking on it, I might eventually need intensive resources from my local hospital that could have been avoided. If nurses were contacting me to make sure I was monitoring my blood pressure, I might never have needed to go into the hospital."[42]

With fewer patients in the hospital, shorter hospital stays, and more medical procedures being done on an outpatient basis, there will be fewer nurses working in hospitals. According to the Bureau of Labor Statistics, the number of hospital nurses is expected to grow by only 17 percent by 2018, compared with 33 percent for home health-care nurses. In addition, as the American population ages, more nurses will be needed in nursing homes and other community settings.

Nurses are seeing a change in their patients in terms of what patients know and what they expect from their health-care providers. Largely because of the Internet, patients are much more informed than they were just twenty years ago about their own health problems and available treatment methods. Patients can research "report cards" on the doctors and hospitals in their community. They know that they have more options than they used to, and they are demanding a larger role in the decisions that are made about their care and how they spend their health-care dollars. For example, since the 1980s there has been rapid growth in the number of patients who ask for complementary and alternative medicine (CAM). CAM is a group of health-care practices and products that are not considered traditional medicine. It includes such things as yoga, dietary supplements, acupuncture, meditation, hypnosis, massage, and many others. Nurses will need to be familiar with these alternative therapies because their patients will be. Nurses and nursing leaders are very optimistic about the ability of nursing to change and grow, and they are confident that the challenges faced in the future can be fully met.

They also know, however, that it will take time and a great deal of work and collaboration with governments, insurance providers, physicians and other health-care providers, and patients. Says Catherine L. Gillis, "There's a need for many hands, and this may be nursing's shining moment."[43]

Notes

Introduction: The Finest Art

1. Quoted in Barbara M. Dossey. *Florence Nightingale: Mystic, Visionary, Healer*. Philadelphia: Lippincott Wilson & Wilkins, 2000, p. 294.
2. Quoted in M. Patricia Donahue. *Nursing, the Finest Art: An Illustrated History*. Maryland Heights, MO: Mosby Elsevier, 2011, p. 1.
3. Mary Ellen Snodgrass. *Historical Encyclopedia of Nursing*. Santa Barbara, CA: ABC-CLIO, 1999, p. xvii.

Chapter One: A Religious Calling

4. Donahue. *Nursing, the Finest Art*, p. 45.
5. Quoted in Donahue. *Nursing, the Finest Art*, p. 56.
6. Mary Adelaide Nutting and Lavinia Lloyd Dock. *A History of Nursing*. Vol. 1. New York: Putnam, 1937, p. 500.

Chapter Two: The Nightingale Revolution

7. Quoted in Donahue. *Nursing, the Finest Art*, p. 116.
8. Donahue. *Nursing, the Finest Art*, p. 116.
9. Florence Nightingale. *Notes on Nursing—What It Is and What It Is Not*. New York: Dover, 1969, p. 8.
10. Nightingale. *Notes on Nursing* p. 12.

11. Quoted in Alex Attewell. "Florence Nightingale." United Nations Educational, Scientific and Cultural Organization. www.ibe.unesco .org/fileadmin/user_upload /archive/publications/Thinkers Pdf/nightingalee.PDF.
12. Quoted in Donahue. *Nursing, the Finest Art*, p. 122.
13. Victor Robinson. *White Caps: The Story of Nursing*. Philadelphia: Lippincott, 1946, p. 129.
14. Quoted in Country Joe McDonald's Tribute to Florence Nightingale. "Florence Nightingale Songs and Poems." www.countryjoe.com /nightingale/broadside.htm.

Chapter Three: Nursing Becomes a Profession

15. Quoted in Donahue. *Nursing, the Finest Art*, p. 141.
16. Quoted in Donahue. *Nursing, the Finest Art*, p. 142.
17. Quoted in Frontier Nursing Service. "How FNS Began—a Brief History of the Frontier Nursing Service." www.frontiernursing.org/History /HowFNSbegan.shtm.
18. Quoted in Frontier Nursing Service. "How FNS Began."
19. Lillian Wald. *The House on Henry Street*. Piscataway, NJ: Transaction, 1991, pp. 4–6.

20. Quoted in Christine Hallett. *Celebrating Nurses: A Visual History*. Hauppauge, NY: Barron's Educational Series, 2010, p. 92.
21. Mary Adelaide Nutting. "Proceedings of the First Meeting of the American Federation of Nurses, Address by the President." *American Journal of Nursing*, July 1905, pp. 654–655.
22. Hallett. *Celebrating Nurses*, p. 95.

Chapter Four: Nurses at War

23. Minnie Goodnow. *Outlines of Nursing History*. Philadelphia: Saunders, 1916, p. 121.
24. Goodnow. *Outlines of Nursing History*, p. 122.
25. Quoted in History Matters. "'This Is How It Was': An American Nurse in France During World War I." http://historymatters.gmu.edu/d/5326.
26. Quoted in Miriam B. Murphy. "Some 80 Nurses Served in World War I." *History Blazer*, September 1995. http://historytogo.utah.gov/utah_chapters/from_war_to_war/some80utahnursesservedinworldwar1.html.
27. Quoted in Snodgrass. *Historical Encyclopedia of Nursing*, p. 285.
28. Donahue. *Nursing, the Finest Art*, p. 204.
29. Mary T. Sarnecky. "The Army Nurse Corps in the Korean War." Korean War 60th Anniversary Fact Sheet. www.koreanwar60.com/army-nurse-corps-korean-war.
30. Donahue. *Nursing, the Finest Art*, p. 212.
31. Quoted in May Peng, Fangzhong Luo, Jacqueline Idun, Arletha Jefferson, Tsewang Yangzom, and Mary Gibson. "The Evolution of War and Nursing." University of Virginia School of Nursing, April 2011. www.virginia.edu/inauguration/posters/2.68.Biosciences.Peng.Luo.Idun.Gibson.pdf.
32. Quoted in Sarnecky. "The Army Nurse Corps in the Korean War."

Chapter Five: Nursing in the Twentieth Century

33. Quoted in Donahue. *Nursing, the Finest Art*, p. 238.
34. Quoted in *Popular Science Monthly*, "Euthanasia," May 1873, pp. 90–91.

Chapter Six: Challenges for the Future

35. Barbara R. Heller, Marla T. Oros, and Jane Durney-Crowley. "The Future of Nursing Education: Ten Trends to Watch." National League for Nursing, 2011. www.nln.org/nlnjournal/infotrends.htm.
36. Quoted in Gerontological Society of America. "Baby Boom Health Care Crisis Looms." Science Daily, April 25, 2008. www.sciencedaily.com/releases/2008/04/080417111300.htm.
37. Quoted in Debra Wood. "Nursing Leaders Reveal Top Trends Impacting Nurses in 2010." NurseZone.com, January 15, 2010. www.nursezone.com/nursing-news-events/more-news/Nursing-Leaders-Reveal-Top-Trends-Impacting-Nurses-in-2010_33230.aspx.
38. Robert Wood Johnson Foundation. *The Future of Nursing: Leading Change, Advancing Health*. Washington, DC: National Academies Press, 2010, p. S-6.

39. Quoted in Wood. "Nursing Leaders Reveal Top Trends Impacting Nurses in 2010."

40. Future of Nursing. "About." http://thefutureofnursing.org/about.

41. Quoted in Pauline W. Chen. "Nurses' Role in the Future of Health Care." *New York Times*, November 18, 2010. www.nytimes.com/2010/11/18/health/views/18chen.html.

42. Quoted in *Rockford (IL) Register Star.* "Nursing Industry Trends to Watch for in 2011 and Beyond," May 5, 2011. www.rrstar.com/healthyrockford/x1471445121/Nursing-industry-trends-to-watch-for-in-2011-and-beyond.

43. Quoted in Chen. "Nurses' Role in the Future of Health Care."

Glossary

beguinage: A group residence for members of the Beguines, a secular nursing order established in the twelfth century.

deaconess: A woman with some education who was selected by the church to provide care to the sick and supervise younger nurses.

ergotism: Also called Saint Anthony's Fire, a disease caused by ingestion of ergot, a toxin in a fungus that affects rye and other cereal grains.

euthanasia: The practice of ending a life in order to end pain and suffering.

feudal system: The European economic system of the Middle Ages in which poverty-stricken serfs farmed land belonging to a wealthy lord.

hospice: A system of physical, emotional, and financial support and care provided to those near the end of life.

hospitallers: Military orders of knights formed during the Crusades to provide care to sick and wounded soldiers and pilgrims.

infectious disease: A disease that can be transmitted from person to person.

matron: A wealthy Roman woman who converted to Christianity and devoted herself to public service, including nursing care.

mendicant orders: Religious orders whose members owned nothing and lived lives of poverty and service, depending totally on the charity of others.

miasmas: A word for bad or polluted air, which was once thought to be the cause of disease before germs were discovered.

midwife: A woman who provides services in childbirth and care of the mother and newborn.

monasteries: Communities in which the members of a religious order live and work.

nosochomia: Patient wards within the *xenodocheia*.

poultice: A soft, moist mass of bread, cereal, or herbs, spread on layers of cloth and applied to the body to relieve pain or inflammation.

secular: Nonreligious or semireligious.

serfs: During the Middle Ages, poverty-stricken peasants who farmed land belonging to a wealthy lord.

vaccine: A medication that is given to prevent a person from catching an infectious disease.

xenodocheia: A Greek word for an early hospital.

For More Information

Books

Christine Hallett. *Celebrating Nurses: A Visual History*. Hauppauge, NY: Barron's Educational Series, 2010. A clearly written and highly illustrated history of nursing from ancient times to the present.

Florence Nightingale. *Notes on Nursing: What It Is and What It Is Not*. New York: Dover, 1969. A reprint of Florence Nightingale's original text about her ideas and philosophy of nursing.

Stuart Ross. *Don't Say No to Flo: The Story of Florence Nightingale*. London: Wayland, 2003. Stories about Florence Nightingale written for younger readers.

Hugh Small. *The Passion of Florence Nightingale*. Stroud, Gloucestershire, England: Amberly, 2010. A biography of Florence Nightingale that presents new information about her life and career.

Mary Ellen Snodgrass. *Historical Encyclopedia of Nursing*. Santa Barbara, CA: ABC-CLIO, 1999. A nursing history arranged alphabetically by topic.

Rosemary Wells. *Mary on Horseback: Three Mountain Stories*. New York: Penguin, 2000. Three stories about Mary Breckinridge and the Frontier Nursing Service, written from the point of view of three fictional people of the time.

Websites

Brownson's Nursing Notes: History (http://diannebrownson.tripod.com/history.html). Dozens of links to various topics in nursing history.

An 1895 Look at Nursing, Emergency Nursing World! (http://enw.org/1895_Nursing.htm). This extract from the 1895 book *Ambulance Work and Nursing—a Handbook on First Aid to the Injured with a Section on Nursing* provides a glimpse of how nursing was viewed at the end of the nineteenth century.

History of Nursing in America: The Ultimate Web Guide, *Nurseblogger* (http://onlinebsn.org/2011/the-history-of-nursing-in-america-the-ultimate-web-guide). Includes links to many sources of information on American nursing history.

Military Nurses in Vietnam (www.illyria.com/vnwnurse.html). A site with links to first-person accounts from nurses who served in the Vietnam War.

Index

recruiting poster for, *57*

CAM (complementary and alternative medicine), 90–91

Childbirth, 43

Christianity, 9
early, nursing and, 12–14

Civil War (1861–1865), 36, 50–53
Union field hospital in, *51*

Cleveland, Emmelin H., 35

Complementary and alternative medicine (CAM), 90–91

Constantine (Roman emperor), 12

Corporal Works of Mercy, 12–13

Crimean War (1853–1856), 30
Mary Seacole and, 33

Crusades, 17–18

Cruzan, Nancy, 78

D

Dark Ages, 14–15

Deaconess Institute at Kaiserworth, 26

Deconesses, 14

Department of Health, Education, and Welfare, U.S., 73

Diagnostic technologies, 67

Dix, Dorothea, 26, 53

DNA, 67

Dock, Lavinia Lloyd, 23

Douglass, Frederick, 54

Dunant, Henri, 31

E

Euthanasia, 75–78

F

Fabiola (Roman matron), 14

Family Limitation (pamphlet), 66

Fenwick, Bedford, 38–39

Fenwick, Ethel, 38, 40, *40*

Ferdinand, Franz, 53

Feudal system, 15

Fliedner, Friederike, 26

Fliedner, Theodor, 26

Francis of Assisi, 19, *19*

Frontier Nursing Service, 43, 44

Fry, Elizabeth Gurney, 25

Future of Nursing: Campaign for Action, 89–90

The Future of Nursing (Robert Wood Johnson Foundation and Institute of Medicine), 88

G

Galen, 9, *10*

Gates, Horatio, 52

Genetic science, 67

Germ theory, 48

Godey's Lady's Book (magazine), *37*

Greece, Ancient, 9

Gregory, Samuel, 43

Gregory IX (pope), 19

Gross, Samuel D., 36–37

H

Harvey, William, 22

Health care
in ancient world, 9
in prehistoric time, 8–9

Health-care reform, 86–87
history of attempts at, 89

Henry Street Settlement, 46–48

Henry VIII (king of England), 23

Picture Credits

Cover: © North Wind Pictures

© Amoret Tanner/Alamy, 33

© AP Images/Bettmann/Corbis, 47, 76, 87

© Bettmann/Corbis, 63

© Bridgeman-Giraudon/Art Resource, NY, 21

© Daily Mail/Rex/Alamy, 40

© DeA Picture Library/Art Resource, NY, 22

© Eliot Elisofon/Time & Life Pictures/Getty Images, 44

© Everett Collection Historical/Alamy, 6, 10, 28, 55

© Floyd W. Gunnison/George Eastman House/Getty Images, 71

© Fotosearch/Getty Images, 51

© Gamma Keystone via Getty Images, 66

© Genevieve Naylor/Corbis, 60

© Getty Images, 84

© GL Archive/Alamy, 29, 32

© Golden Pixels, LLC/Alamy, 80

© Historical image collection by Bildagentur-online/Alamy, 6

© Hulton Archive/Getty Images, 39, 57, 74

© Image Asset Management Ltd./Alamy, 54

© Juice Images/Alamy, 83

© Lebrecht Music and Arts Photo Library/Alamy, 16

© The Museum of the City of New York/Art Resource, NY, 42

© Niday Picture Library/Alamy, 6

© Norma Jean Gargasz/Alamy, 70

© North Wind Picture Archives/Alamy, 6

© PAP Images/The Wenatchee World, Kelly Gillin, 69

© Paul Morris/Time Life Pictures/Getty Images, 85

© Prisma/UIG/Getty Images, 19

© Snark/Art Resource, NY, 18

© Trinity Mirror/Mirropix/Alamy, 7

© UIG via Getty Images, 13

© Universal History Archive/Getty Images, 25

© Women's ward in the Middlesex Hospital, London. From The Microcosm of London, Ackermann, London, 1808 -11. Illustrated by Pugin and Rowlandson. Aquatint/Universal History Archive/UIG/The Bridgeman Art Library, 36

About the Author

Lizabeth Craig lives in Springfield, Missouri, and has been a surgical nurse for thirty-two years. She received her nursing degree from the University of Florida and a teaching degree from Southwest Missouri State University. She enjoys writing for children and adults, especially on topics in history and medicine. *History of Nursing* is her eleventh book for Lucent Books.